photographing

London

Amphoto
Travel
Guide

photographing
London

Albert Moldvay
Erika Fabian

Amphoto
American Photographic
Book Publishing Co., Inc.

NEW YORK, NEW YORK

Acknowledgements
Our thanks to Pan American World Airways, Agfa Gevaert, Vivitar,
The British Tourist Authority, and personally to Len Rees for their help
and cooperation.

All photographs by the authors
Design by The Graphic Image
Maps by Arnold Bombay

Library of Congress Cataloging in Publication Data

Moldvay, Albert, 1921-
    Photographing London.

    (Amphoto travel guide)
    Includes index.
    1.   Travel photography.   2.   London.   I.   Fabian,
Erika, joint author.   II.   Title.
TR790.M64   778.9'9'94210857   79-25866

ISBN 0-8174-2125-4

Manufactured in the United States of America

Contents

ABOUT THE SYMBOLS

The numbered arrows on the maps are guides to show good locations for camera viewpoints. Symbols are used to rate the *visual importance* of each sight.

Three symbols mean that it is a *not-to-be-missed* picture.

Two symbols indicate that you should try for it but not at the expense of the "not-to-be-missed sights."

One symbol tells you, "this is another location that will make a good photograph."

One of the problems of photographing in a big city is that a sight is often missed simply because you didn't know it was there. We suggest that you follow the *Guide* and then return to other picture possibilities you may have seen along the way.

1. Things You Should Know About London

London is snug, home-like, and intimate. Photographing this city is like shooting for your family picture album.

It's snug because all the major sights are around the bend on the Thames River where London originally started. You don't have to go long distances from sight to sight, or from one picturable district to another.

London is home-like to Americans and anyone familiar with English history. A trip through Westminster Abbey, a visit to the Tower of London, and a look at Big Ben are all reminders of lessons and literature that you have studied.

The intimacy of London is reflected in its many squares and individual districts with club-like pubs and cozy restaurants, each having its own characteristic flavor.

London is not a city of grand vistas like Paris, or grand ruins like Rome. The streets, except for a few main thoroughfares, are short and narrow. Driving in the city is a constant discovery of squares and parks that interrupt the flow of traffic. Yet it is not a colorful scene, and perhaps in recognition of this, the English have injected pomp and pageantry. The Changing of the Guard at Buckingham Palace and the Beefeater guards at the Tower of London are everyday examples.

The best pictorial approach to London is first to cover the suggested sights and pageants, and then wander around in the various sections and capture the individual flavor.

THE BEST PICTURE TIME TO GO

The stereotyped picture of the Londoner striding along with his everpresent umbrella is based on fact—the fact that the weather is so changeable, you never know when the next rain will fall. There's not much you can do about the weather but take your chances, and take along some high-speed film for those dark days.

Colorful pushcarts may be found right in the downtown section. For identification, try to tie them to the local scene—in this case, the red double-decker buses.

*Tower Bridge is most interest-
ing when it opens up to let
ships through.*

London's best visiting time is the same as the rest of the continent: summer and fall. Photographically too, these are the best times, because you'll find flowers blooming in the many parks, and people mingling at street fairs and relaxing at the occasional sidewalk cafes.

Buildings photograph best in sunlight; but, as noted above, you may run into a series of cloudy and rainy days in London. Use these bad-weather days to photograph interiors. WESTMINSTER ABBEY, THE BRITISH MUSEUM, and the TOWER OF LONDON all have interesting subjects for photography inside.

CURRENT EVENTS

There are many events and festivals, and a lot of entertainment in London which may be scheduled during your stay. Some of these happenings make good pictures and will give you a chance to add to your photo collection.

A quick reference list to current happenings appears in *London Week,* which you can pick up at most hotels or at the BRITISH TOURIST AUTHORITY at 64 ST. JAMES'S STREET, LONDON SW1 (TEL: 01-499-9325) or the LONDON TOURIST BOARD at 26 GROSVENOR GARDENS, LONDON SW1 (TEL: 01-730-0791), or VICTORIA STATION opposite platform 15, SELFRIDGES, HARROD'S, THE TOWER OF LONDON, HEATHROW CENTRAL STATION, and the CITY OF LONDON INFORMATION CENTER at St. Paul's Church Yard. You can also call 01-246-8041 for a recorded message of the day's events in London.

CUSTOMS AND RESTRICTIONS ON PHOTOGRAPHY

There are no restrictions on the number of cameras or the amount of film that you can take to Great Britain, and there are very few restrictions on photographing in general. (You can even take pictures from a private plane without special permission.)

If there are any restrictions on the London scene, you will be informed. (The National Gallery and the Tate, for example, do not permit photography, whereas the British Museum does.) You cannot photograph a performance in a theater with or without flash, and they clearly post this prohibition.

But there are times when special arrangements are made just for photographers, such as **Photographers' Night** in **Westminster Abbey**.

Burlington Arcade is like a glass-enclosed street, lined with charming bow-windowed shops. It is a delightful place to photograph in any weather.

PICTURABLE FESTIVALS

The outdoor street fairs are a colorful addition to the London scene. There, the locals mix with the recently arrived visitors from the Arab countries and former British colonies. These well-known fairs are held in various locations during the summer and are listed in the biweekly magazine *London Week* published by the BRITISH TOURIST AUTHORITY.

Beside the changing happenings there are some yearly scheduled events that make good pictures. Here is a list that you should keep in mind:

February
CRUFT'S DOG SHOW at OLYMPIA EXHIBITION HALL (call 01-493-6651 for information). Over 9,000 dogs are exhibited, representing 140 breeds. If you're a dog lover, you shouldn't miss this one.

March
SPRING ANTIQUES FAIR at CHELSEA OLD TOWN HALL. Some 40 exhibitors display all types of antique jewelry, furniture, instruments, and icons. A good picture-hunting expedition, even if you can't afford to buy. Call ST. ALBANS 56069 for information from the antique dealers.

Easter
Two picture possibilities are the CARNIVAL PARADE on Easter Sunday in BATTERSEA PARK and the LONDON HARNESS HORSE PARADE the following Monday morning in REGENT'S PARK.

April
The ROYAL HORTICULTURAL SOCIETY SPRING FLOWER SHOW should give you opportunities to photograph colorful flowers and some colorful candids of the flower lovers.

May
The ROYAL WINDSOR HORSE SHOW is a chance to take some classy horse events including the mounted band of the HOUSEHOLD CAVALRY. Call 01-637-3131 for tickets and reservations.

May
CHELSEA FLOWER SHOW. Another major flower show held at CHELSEA ROYAL HOSPITAL. For information call the ROYAL HORTICULTURAL SOCIETY at 01-834-4333.

BEATING RETREAT, massed bands of the ROYAL MARINES at the HORSE GUARDS PARADE at WHITEHALL — for tickets call 01-839-6815.

June
TROOPING THE COLOR — THE QUEEN'S BIRTHDAY PARADE. It is difficult to get tickets for the actual parade but there are two rehearsals before, one on May 20th and another on May 27th. (The first rehearsal is free but you will need tickets for the second.) Write to H.Q. Household Division, Horse Guards, Whitehall London, SW 1 2AX, before March 1st. for reservations.

July
OPEN AIR THEATER SEASON in REGENT'S PARK. Check the Tourist Board or the *London Week* publication for times and shows here as well as several other outdoor entertainments held during July.

Check also for dates on the DOGGET'S COAT AND BADGE ROWING RACE from LONDON BRIDGE to CHELSEA BRIDGE — a chance for some river activity with the PARLIAMENT or other prominent river shore buildings in the background (this one is usually held the last Friday in the month).

July
ROYAL TOURNAMENT MALL MARCH. Another chance to take shots of the British Armed Forces along THE MALL from Buckingham Palace to Trafalgar Square.

July
ROYAL TOURNAMENT at EARLS COURT. A mix of military bands, cavalry, and exotic Gurkha and Hong Kong detachments ending with a fireworks display—all good photo material.

July
ROYAL INTERNATIONAL HORSE SHOW at WEMBLEY ARENA. This is a night event but you'll be able to get shots with high speed indoor film (see the "Tips and Techniques" section on Show Shooting).

Also on July 17th is the CITY OF LONDON FESTIVAL which includes various events that you can picture with the historic old buildings in the background.

July
SWAN-UPPING. The annual marking of swans owned by the queen and the guilds. This event takes place along the THAMES from Kingston to Henley.

August
In August there are a series of fairs held in London, the chief of which is the fair at HAMPSTEAD HEATH. These are good events for candids and people activity.

GREATER LONDON HORSE SHOW at CLAPHAM COMMON— another chance to picture the horsy types.

SUMMER FLOWER SHOW at the ROYAL HORTICULTURAL SOCIETY in WESTMINSTER and the OUTDOOR THEATER SEASON in HOLLAND PARK. Both good people-watching events.

September
CHELSEA ANTIQUES FAIR. Another big antique event.

October
A PROCESSION OF JUDGES IN FULL ROBES at WESTMINSTER ABBEY to open the Michaelmas Law Term. Check the Tourist Bureau for date.

November
LONDON TO BRIGHTON VETERAN CAR RUN held on the first Sunday of the month. A good chance for shots of antique cars.

December
(About the middle of the month.) The lighting of the Christmas tree in TRAFALGAR SQUARE.

Two year-round spectacles held daily, that you don't want to miss, are the CHANGING OF THE GUARD AT BUCKINGHAM PALACE at 11:30 A.M. and the HORSE GUARDS PARADE AT WHITEHALL at 11:00 A.M. daily, and 10:00 A.M. on Sundays. Both of these are top photo attractions of London.

TAKING CARE OF YOUR EQUIPMENT AND YOURSELF

London, like all major cities, has a crime problem and you should take this into consideration. Be careful with your camera, as well as other personal possessions. Don't put your camera bag down on the sidewalk while you turn around for another view, and don't leave your camera exposed inside a car, even if it is locked.

Pickpockets work not only on the streets, but inside the major stores. In fact, we were startled in Selfridge's by an announcement warning customers that "pickpockets are now working" at one of the entrances.

Be especially careful when shooting night illumination pictures, because places like Piccadilly Circus and the Theater District are known hangouts for thieves. Don't let the reassuring sight of "bobbies" patrolling lull you into a false sense of security.

Sir Thomas More's statue is typical of the many memorials to famous men to be found around London.

*Look for contrasting details of
new and old. Here, a modern
street traffic sign adds color
and contrast to an old ship's
anchor device.*

WHERE TO BUY FILM AND HAVE IT
DEVELOPED

Buying and having film developed in London is just about
the same as in the States as to prices and availability. There are
two well-known names that you should keep in mind concerning
anything photographic: one is **WALLACE HEATON,** and the other
is **DIXON'S.** Both of these stores are located on New Bond
Street, right in the center of London, off Oxford Street. Dixon's
has branches in other parts of London as well.

Labs take about ten days to develop film. So on a short
trip it's much better to bring your film with you and wait until you
get home to have it developed.

WHERE TO BUY EQUIPMENT AND HAVE YOUR CAMERA REPAIRED

Dixon's and Wallace Heaton are two good places to look for equipment, but if you're bargain-hunting, other stores will have better prices on some items. In any case, don't plan to buy in London unless you really need something because the prices are higher than, say, New York City, where you can get some real bargains.

The same holds true for camera repairs. One recommended repair shop is **SENDEAN LTD.**, 6-7 D'Arblay Street, London W.1., Tel: 439-8418. They handle all brands, but repair there takes an estimated six weeks. In addition to the repair charge, there is a £2.00 charge for the estimate if you refuse the repair.

Again, repair and equipment are in the same category as film and development: Try to hold off until you get back from your trip. But if you do run into trouble, you will surely be helped with typical British courtesy.

The view from the top of the Monument, erected to the memory of the Great Fire of London, is one of the few high places to get an overall view of the City of London.

Commonplace details such as the "look right" traffic sign, can make interesting shots.

THE BEST WAY TO GET AROUND LONDON

Bus tours, or as the English say, "coach tours," are the best way to see London and to get a good overall idea of the sights. After the tour, you can revisit the places that looked interesting.

Bus Tours

There are two types of bus tours. The relatively inexpensive one is a LONDON TRANSPORT tour, which takes about two hours. These buses leave from GROSVENOR GARDENS, VICTORIA STATION, PICCADILLY CIRCUS and MARBLE ARCH, on the hour, starting at 10 A.M. You simply queue up and get on. The trick is to wait for the open-top buses, because they make excellent shooting platforms for picture-taking. The other type of bus tour is more extensive. There are two half-day conducted tours: one in the morning, and one in the afternoon. You should take both to get a good overall look at the city. Some stops are included, such as, ST. PAUL'S CATHEDRAL, THE TOWER OF LONDON, and the ALBERT MEMORIAL. For information on these conducted tours, contact the BRITISH TOURIST AUTHORITY, or the LONDON TOURIST BOARD.

London Taxi Guides

A new guide service that seems to be tailor-made for photography is the LONDON TAXI GUIDES. They are a group of taxi drivers who are also licensed guides and use their taxis for personal tours. The cost for a day's conducted taxi tour is about the same as the price of four adult bus-tour tickets. But the taxi will take four people comfortably, so if you can make up a photographic foursome it will not cost you any more.

The definite advantage of the taxi tour over the bus is that you can hop out any time you see something you want to photograph, and the taxi will wait for you. You can even plan the day's itinerary to take advantage of the right time of day for the best light.

The taxi guides can be contacted through the LONDON TOURIST BOARD, or call: 01-542-4355.

The Underground

If you know London well enough to get around by yourself, the cheapest and fastest way is to take the underground to the major points of interest and walk or take a taxi from there.

2. London's Most Picturable Sights and Events

There are some sights in London that you absolutely shouldn't miss. In fact, if you're on a short trip and you go directly to these places and events, you will have a good collection of London photos.

THE CHANGING OF THE GUARD AT BUCKINGHAM PALACE AND THE HORSE GUARDS PARADE AT WHITEHALL

These two events are the best known in London, and you can combine the two and double your picture-take because the Horse Guards ride past Buckingham Palace from their barracks to the Horse Guards Parade at Whitehall. Since they have to be at Whitehall by 11 A.M. and the guard change at Buckingham is at 11:30 A.M., you can photograph HORSE GUARDS as they pass by, and remain for the CHANGING OF THE GUARD.

A good view of Buckingham Palace may be photographed from in front of the Queen Victoria statue. Include the statue as well for foreground interest.

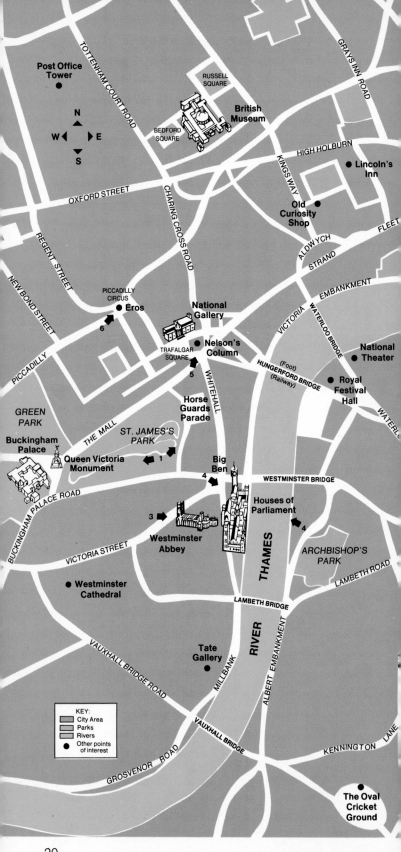

Post Office Tower

RUSSELL SQUARE

British Museum

BEDFORD SQUARE

HIGH HOLBURN

Lincoln's Inn

Old Curiosity Shop

N
W E
S

TOTTENHAM COURT ROAD

KINGSWAY

ALDWYCH

FLEET

STRAND

OXFORD STREET

CHARING CROSS ROAD

EMBANKMENT

REGENT STREET

NEW BOND STREET

PICCADILLY CIRCUS
Eros
6

National Gallery

VICTORIA

WATERLOO BRIDGE

GRAYS INN ROAD

National Theater

TRAFALGAR SQUARE

Nelson's Column

5

(Foot)
HUNGERFORD BRIDGE
(Railway)

Royal Festival Hall

PICCADILLY

WHITEHALL

Horse Guards Parade

WATERLO

GREEN PARK

THE MALL

ST. JAMES'S PARK

1

Big Ben
4

Buckingham Palace

Queen Victoria Monument

BUCKINGHAM PALACE ROAD

WESTMINSTER BRIDGE

3

Westminster Abbey

Houses of Parliament

4

ARCHBISHOP'S PARK

LAMBETH ROAD

VICTORIA STREET

THAMES

Westminster Cathedral

LAMBETH BRIDGE

VAUXHALL BRIDGE ROAD

Tate Gallery

RIVER

MILLBANK

ALBERT EMBANKMENT

KEY:
City Area
Parks
Rivers
● Other points of interest

VAUXHALL BRIDGE

GROSVENOR ROAD

KENNINGTON LANE

The Oval Cricket Ground

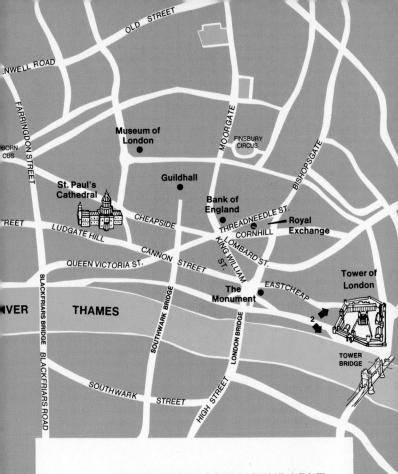

LONDON'S MOST PICTURABLE SIGHTS AND EVENTS

1. The Changing of the Guard at Buckingham Palace, and the Horse Guards Parade at Whitehall—the most colorful photographic event in London.

2. The Tower of London and Tower Bridge—a photogenic look into the grisly past.

3. Westminster Abbey—where kings, statesmen, and poets are buried. Photography is permitted on Wednesday evenings.

4. Big Ben and the Houses of Parliament—the best views and how to take them.

5. Trafalgar Square—how to "square up" Nelson's Column, and what to shoot around the square.

6. Piccadilly Circus, where Eros poses, disguised as the "angel of heavenly virtue."

The mounted Horse Guards can be photographed in action as they trot from Buckingham Palace to Whitehall. Use the prefocusing technique and shoot when the troop is in range.

The Horse Guards

To make sure that you get the Horse Guards riding by, it is best to be standing at the **MALL ENTRANCE** to the **VICTORIA MEMORIAL** in front of **BUCKINGHAM PALACE** by 10:30 A.M. You can fill in the waiting time by taking some shots of the **VICTORIA MEMORIAL** with the **PALACE** in the background, from the semi-circular gardens, facing this view. For added height, step up onto the low wall that borders the gardens, and take in the entire scene with a wide-angle lens. Focus on the monument, and your image will be sharp all the way to the Palace. Include the flowers in your pictures to add color.

The Mall, which runs between Buckingham Palace and Trafalgar Square, is the best place to take shots of the mounted Horse Guards as they trot from their barracks to Whitehall. They make a better picture here because they are in motion, rather than at Whitehall where they just stand still during the guard change.

Plan your view before they arrive, prefocus, and wait for them to appear. They take the road that runs along the north side of the Palace, past the Victoria Memorial, and turn onto the Mall. Just before they reach Trafalgar Square, they turn south to Whitehall.

A moderately long telephoto lens (80–135 mm) will compress the perspective so that the troops will seem closer together. This focal length is suggested because a shorter lens will separate them and a longer telephoto is hard to keep in focus or steady. Remember to increase your shutter speed to 1/250 or 1/500 sec. to stop the action of the riders.

The guards ride at a slow trot so you will have time to take more than one shot. To shoot a series, start with your longest telephoto and change lenses as they move closer.

You can obtain a good view of the marching bands leaving Buckingham Palace when they round the statue of Queen Victoria. Prefocus on the statue and wait for the formation to march into focus.

The Changing of the Guard at Buckingham Palace

After photographing the Horse Guards walk back to the Victoria Memorial. Here you can get a clear view of the gate where the Guards exit after the changing ceremony that takes place within the enclosed courtyard. During the changing, you can't go inside, because the gates are closed. It is possible to shoot through the iron fence, but you have to be there very early, before the crowds start to gather. (Actually it's not a good idea to stand next to the fence, because you won't be able to get through the throngs of people when the Guards make their exit through the gate. And the police will not let you cross the road to change your viewpoint.)

Don't stand in the front row of spectators facing the Palace from the island where the Victoria Memorial is located. Walk up the steps so that you can shoot over the heads of the rest of the tourists and get some additional height for a better view.

The regiments march out in two formations, each led by a band. One of these groups turns to the right and the other to the left as they march through the gate, so you can get a picture from either side. Focus on the gate and get your photo when they come out. Then shift your viewpoint so that the Palace is in the background, refocus, and get another picture as they march by. A normal lens is just about right for the views from the stairway, showing the guards marching by with the Palace in the background.

The Mounted Sentries

After you have taken the pictures of the Changing of the Guard, you can go to the front of the **HORSE GUARDS** building on **WHITEHALL** and take close-ups of the mounted sentries sitting on their horses on each side of the entry gate. These guards have to remain as still as statues, so you can take your time and get some excellent close-ups.

The mounted sentries can be photographed while they are on guard duty. A telephoto lens brings them portrait close without disturbing them.

*A classic view of the Tower
from the Thames River entry.
This view can be taken from
the esplanade along the river
bank.*

THE TOWER OF LONDON AND THE TOWER BRIDGE

There are good picture opportunities both outside and inside the TOWER walls.

Outside the Tower Walls

The best outside views are from the park and walkway along the Thames right by the TOWER BRIDGE. The view from there shows the turrets of the BLOODY TOWER with the WHITE TOWER in the background, while in the foreground there is a row of cannons lined up on the parkway. From along this walkway you can also get some good shots of the Tower Bridge; and if you're in luck, a large boat may pass by under the opened spans. The light for this shot is best in the afternoon, so do the Tower tour first and then take the shots along the river.

The best views of the
historic Tower Bridge are
from the park and walkway
along the Thames. *The light
for this shot is best in the
afternoon.*

The Beefeater guides at the
Tower of London make in-
teresting subjects as they
gesture and explain the Tower's history. Just photograph
them as you listen.

Another good outside view is from where you stand in line waiting to enter the Tower complex. A wide-angle lens will take in the walls and the White Tower behind as well as the MIDDLE TOWER, through which you enter the grounds.

If you're not with a tour guide, it's best to take one of the guided BEEFEATER TOURS. This way you get some of the Tower history, as well as a chance to take some shots of the Beefeater guide himself. While following the inside tour, keep an eye out for the RAVENS that walk about. They are part of the Tower lore, and you can get some close-ups with a telephoto lens.

Inside the Tower Walls

The views within the Tower can best be taken with a wide-angle lens because you are right among the tall walls of the buildings and there is no room to back up.

The changing of the guards in front of the WATERLOO BARRACKS can best be taken from the wooden staircase that leads to the upper floor of the WHITE TOWER. From this elevation, you can straighten the vertical lines of the barracks and take in the guard change as well.

St. Peter's Chapel. The Beefeater guide will take you inside ST. PETER'S CHAPEL, where there are some opportunities for inside views of the altar and the tombs where notables are buried. The light is dim, but by supporting your camera against the columns and the walls, you can make slow, handheld (but supported) exposures of up to 1 sec. If you are using high-speed film, and the shutter speeds fall within 1/15th sec. or faster, bracing your hand or the side of your arm will be sufficient to steady the camera. But if the exposures are below 1/15 sec., you must brace the camera solidly against a firm support and use the self-timer to release the shutter so that you don't accidentally jar the camera when pushing down on the shutter-release button.

The chapel on the Tower of London grounds is part of the tour. Sunlight filtering through the windows provides enough illumination for interior views.

The armor collection in the
Tower is worth photographing. Use the corrective filters
recommended in the text for
fluorescent lighting.

The White Tower. The main attraction inside the WHITE
TOWER is the ARMOR COLLECTION. The armor is displayed in
glass cases and is well-illuminated by fluorescent fixtures,
which on color film produce a sickly green color. You can correct the color balance by using a corrective filter such as a
Tiffen FLD or FLB, or by flashing. If you choose to flash, be sure
that the camera and light aren't reflected on the glass surface; if
they are, you will "wipe out" the subject with a flash reflection.
You can avoid this problem by moving to the side so that you
don't see your reflection.

New Armories and the Royal Fusiliers Museum. There
are additional shots you can take in the NEW ARMORIES BUILD-
ING and the ROYAL FUSILIERS MUSEUM. There you will find in-

Some of the instruments of torture are displayed and lighted well enough for photography. You can take some quick shots while waiting in the line of spectators.

struments of torture, oriental armor, and other unusual objects, like a model of an elephant, encased in armor. These displays are spotlighted and you should use a high-speed indoor film, for example, Ektachrome 160 film (tungsten). If you don't have tungsten film, you can convert your daylight film by using an 80B filter over the lens. (Two filters you should carry at all times are the 80B to convert daylight film to tungsten, and the 85B to convert tungsten film to daylight.)

An unusual object in the Tower collection is this elephant completely encased in armor. This can be photographed with the exhibit lighting if you support your camera against a nearby showcase.

A spectacular view of Parliament from across the Thames. Here, the roses were used for foreground color and interest. A wide-angle lens will enable you to keep both the flowers and the far scene in sharp focus.

BIG BEN AND THE HOUSES OF PARLIAMENT

The best views of the **HOUSES OF PARLIAMENT** are from across the **THAMES RIVER**, between **LAMBETH** and **WESTMINSTER BRIDGES**.

Across the River

A good overall view can be taken in the morning from the **ALBERT EMBANKMENT**, along which there is a walkway between the two bridges. There is a rose garden along there, which provides good foreground color.

All-in-focus shot. You can try several techniques for this shot. One is to move close to the flower bed and, stopping down your lens, take an all-in-focus picture of the foreground flowers and the spires of the **PARLIAMENT BUILDINGS** across the river. A wide-angle lens is necessary to give you enough depth of field. Instead of focusing on the nearby flowers or the faraway buildings, you should use the technique of zone focusing by using the depth-of-field markings on your lens. (Refer to the "Tips and Techniques" section on how to use the depth-of-field scale for focusing.)

Blurred foreground shots. Another effect is to open up the lens and focus on the distant Parliament buildings so that the foreground is an out-of-focus mass of color. Use a large f-stop, such as f/2.8, and adjust the shutter speed to correspond. If the highest shutter speed, for example, 1/1000 sec., still indicates overexposure, then readjust the f-stop. The preview button on your lens is very useful to see how the blobs of color will look at the taking aperture. Move your camera closer, farther away, and up and down to see how the foreground appears in front of the buildings until you "see" the composition you want.

The **ALBERT EMBANKMENT** has iron light poles with sculptured dolphins on them. These sculpture pieces also make a good foreground for the Parliament view. Move close to one of the pieces and include the Parliament in the background.

This technique of enlarging a subject in the foreground and including a scene in the back, is a good composition device. If you have a wide-angle lens, it's surprisingly easy to take such a picture. For example, with a 24 mm lens, you can be in focus from less than 3 feet to infinity by stopping down to f/22. So don't be afraid to move in close with a wide-angle lens; just be sure that the near and far distances fall within the depth-of-field scale on your lens.

River Traffic. River traffic can also provide pictorial interest. Watch for boats and be ready before they arrive. For best composition, frame your view where you want a boat to be in the picture and shoot when it arrives at that location.

Don't overlook people as foreground possibilities. We took a picture of a class of school children visiting from Hong Kong, complete with banners in Chinese writing, right on the Embankment, with the Parliament in the background.

A night view of the Houses of Parliament is easy to take from across the Thames. Exposures on scenes like this should be bracketed from 1 sec. to 5 sec. at f/2 on slow color film, and from ½ sec. to 3 sec. at f/2 for the fast (ASA 200 to 400) films.

Big Ben can be photographed at night from the park directly facing it. Use the light poles or trees to support your camera for the 1-sec. or longer exposures that are required. (See the photo caption on page 31 for details.)

Nighttime. Daylight is not the only time to take this scene; you can also shoot it at night. A good view is across Westminster Bridge. By the **LONDON COUNTY HALL**, there is a convenient balcony from where you can take in the bridge, a huge stone lion on the bridge approach, and the illuminated towers with **BIG BEN** clearly showing.

A tripod is handy for time exposure, but you don't really need one because you can support the camera right on the stone wall overlooking the scene. Take a meter reading through your lens for the exposure, and bracket; that is, make additional exposures both more and less than the indicated setting to make sure that you have a good one. Bracketing is necessary in shots like this because there is a great difference in the amount of exposure needed between capturing just the lights themselves and the scene that is illuminated by the lights. If you don't have a meter, or it doesn't register low light levels, use our "guesstimated" exposures of 1, 2, and 4 sec. at *f*/2 with ASA 64 daylight color film; and 1/2, 1, and 2 sec. at *f*/2 with high-speed daylight color film of ASA 200. (See "Tips and Techniques" for more on bracketing.)

A normal lens is just about right to take in the view across the Thames, but you will need a wide-angle to include the lion in your composition.

BIG BEN can also be taken at night from the **PARLIAMENT SQUARE**, where the **STATUE OF CHURCHILL** is located. Here again, a night shot is more effective than a day-view, because the clock glows like a jewel on color film. Use the same exposures as for the view over the Thames, and the iron light poles for camera support if you don't have a tripod. A medium-telephoto lens, such as a 105 mm, will give you good close-ups of the clock and tower from the far end of the park facing Big Ben. The added distance will help straighten the vertical lines of the tower.

32

WESTMINSTER ABBEY

WESTMINSTER ABBEY contains the "visual" history of England, and as such, it is a photographic *must*. Since it is so popular with photographers, the Abbey has set aside Wednesday evenings from 6 to 8 P.M. as PHOTOGRAPHER'S NIGHT. At this time, pictures are permitted under the supervision of official volunteer wardens.

The Interior
The late hour doesn't mean that you won't have enough light. And during the summer season, the evening is ideal, because the main rose window over the entrance catches the light of the setting sun. Some parts of the Abbey are dark, but tripods and

The Morris dancers in the foreground add human interest to this view of Westminster Abbey. Look for activities like this when shooting overall scenes.

When shooting stained-glass windows, such as this one in Westminster Abbey, take a direct meter reading through the window area for full color saturation.

flash are permitted. If you plan to take advantage of this picture-taking opportunity, be sure to take at least a small tabletop tripod with you and a flash as well.

The Nave. The first photo view is from the center of the nave facing the main door and the overhead stained-glass window with your back against the choir stalls. From this position you can take a general view of the interior. A wide-angle lens will take in the entire view but a normal lens will also cover it.

34

The backlighted window will give you a bright spot in the center of your frame, which will throw off the exposure reading for the overall scene. To prevent underexposure, aim your camera to the side of the window to get your meter reading from a middle-toned area; then return to the original framing for your picture.

Poet's Corner. The center of the Abbey, along POETS' CORNER, provides good photo material. A particularly good angle is from the back of the choir stalls, shooting through the pews, which are lighted by small lamps with red shades. These red lights against the blue damask cloth on the backs of the pews, along with the gilded woodwork, make a colorful scene.

The Choir. You can take a number of shots: One view with a wide-angle lens takes in the choir in the foreground and the main rose window in the background; or with a normal lens, you can compose the red lamps against the blue cloth and the gold woodwork.

Your flash can be useful when the light level is too low, or when there is a dark scene in the foreground and a light one, such as a stained-glass window, in the background. But don't use flash alone; combine it with the lighting on the scene.

The way to shoot a combination flash/natural-light picture is to first determine your exposure for the existing-light scene; then simply add your flash to it. The flash will give just enough additional light to accent the highlights and lighten the dark shadows; it won't change the middle tones. This technique won't work all the time. If the foreground is close to the camera, the flash will overexpose it and "wash out" the color. It's not effective either if the scene is so far away that the flash doesn't reach it.

The Poet's Corner in the Abbey makes a particularly good shot when streams of sunlight accent the statuary.

A good view down the nave toward the Abbey's main entrance includes the choir loft above.

The choir decorations are colorful details to watch for on the Westminster Abbey photo tour. Use a nearby pew to support your camera for the exposure.

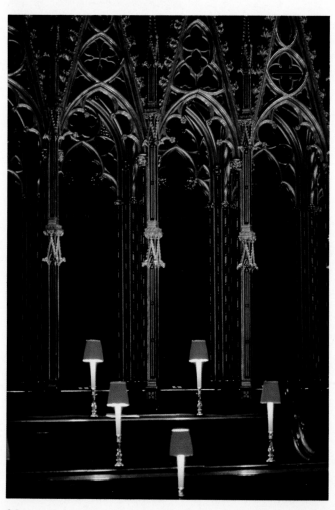

There are several compositions in this central area where you can use the combination flash/natural-light technique. For the choir shot, first take a meter reading (it should be about 1 sec. at *f*/2.8 to *f*/4 on ASA 64 color film) and add your flash. The flash, by the way, will synchronize at any shutter speed slower than the recommended X- synchronization of 1/30 to 1/125 sec.; therefore, at 1 sec., you will get the full additional light of the flash.

Coronation Altar. Another picture that can be taken with flash plus natural light is the CORONATION ALTAR in back of the choir section. In this case, do just the reverse. First determine your *f*-stop setting for the flash, or if you have an auto unit like the Vivitar 283, just set it for the correct *f*-stop range; then slow your shutter down to 1 sec., but keep the *f*-stop setting for your flash. The result will be a well-exposed flash shot with added lighting on the scene.

The Shrine of Edward the Confessor, the Coronation Chair, and the Stone of Scone. The SHRINE OF EDWARD THE CONFESSOR is behind the Coronation Altar and holds the CORONATION CHAIR with the STONE OF SCONE beneath it. This shot should be taken from the side where the sword and shield of Edward are displayed. The best way to shoot this scene is with flash, because you are close-up. But if you don't have a flash, use high-speed tungsten film or an 85B filter to convert your daylight film to tungsten.

The Coronation Altar in Westminster Abbey can be photographed easily with on-camera flash during the photo tour. See the text for details.

There are many chances for colorful shots during a visit to the tombs of Westminster. This red lion stands at the foot of the sarcophagus of Queen Elizabeth I.

The Coronation Chair, with the Stone of Scone beneath it, is best photographed from the side. Use flash if possible, as you will be shooting close-up.

The flags hanging in the Henry VII Chapel are good color subjects inside Westminster Abbey. These can be photographed on the photo tour.

Henry VII Chapel and Battle of Britain Chapel. Farther on toward the back of the Abbey there are two more colorful scenes that you shouldn't miss: The first is the **HENRY VII CHAPEL** with banners lining the walls; and the second shot is the **BATTLE OF BRITAIN CHAPEL**, lighted by a stained-glass window that displays the squadron insignias of the R.A.F. groups that defended London in World War II.

The lighting in the Henry VII Chapel is very dim, and the flags are so high up that a flash would be ineffective. The best technique is to use daylight color film and brace your camera against a column or doorway to steady it for the long exposure. (If you don't have a meter, try f/2.8 at 1 sec. on ASA 64 film, or f/2.8 at 1/4 sec. on high-speed daylight color film (ASA 200 to 400). Make added exposures at more and less time, for safety.)

The focal point of the Battle of Britain Chapel is the **STAINED-GLASS WINDOW**. To expose correctly for the window, simply take a meter reading through your lens. If you want to show the interior of the Chapel as well, use the combination flash and daylight technique by adding flash to the exposure reading.

There are many more subjects for interesting photos in the side chapels where kings and aristocrats are entombed. Use the techniques of braced camera exposures, flash, or a combination of flash and natural light for these shots as well.

TRAFALGAR SQUARE

A good overall shot of **TRAFALGAR SQUARE** is from the **ADMIRALTY ARCH**, which is at the entry to the Mall that leads to Buckingham Palace. From there you can take in **NELSON'S COLUMN**, as well as the **NATIONAL GALLERY** and **ST. MARTIN'S CHURCH** in the background. If you have a telephoto, this is also a good place to take some close-up shots of the **NELSON STATUE**. Move closer and you will have a chance for some good compositions, with the fountains and the statuary as foreground interests. Note especially the two huge lion statues; they are a favorite place for clambering youngsters, who make good candid shots.

Another view is from the terrace in front of the National Gallery, looking down into the **SQUARE**. There are other possibilities for photos as you walk around.

The Nelson Monument in Trafalgar Square is much too tall for close-ups. Move back on such scenes and take in the overall view for identification of place.

Move in close to the fountain and use it as a center of interest for a shot of Trafalgar Square.

CHARING CROSS

Across from Trafalgar Square is the **CHARING CROSS**, which looks like a steeple set in the ground. This is another interesting sight, and offers a chance to take candids of flower vendors and other activity at the same time.

PICCADILLY CIRCUS

This is the "Times Square" of London, and just like its counterpart, it looks better at night than in the daytime.

Daytime
As with **TRAFALGAR SQUARE**, try to shoot **PICCADILLY CIRCUS** on a sunny day, because this scene too has very little color, and the added sunlight is needed.

Nighttime
The best viewpoint for the night shot is from the stairs leading down to the underground, right at the Piccadilly entry. From there, you will be looking up Shaftesbury Avenue, where the lights of the Theater District provide a colorful background.
There are several techniques for this shot.

Piccadilly Circus is best photographed about noon or at quitting time, when the base of the Eros Statue becomes a meeting place for the young. Choose a viewpoint that shows the statue standing out clearly against the sky, rather than looking pasted onto the surrounding buildings.

Technique 1. One is to use Ektachrome 400 film (daylight), with the aperture set at *f*/2.8 (if you open the lens all the way, to *f*/1.4, for example, you will not have enough depth of field for the scene) and adjust the shutter speed according to your meter. You should be able to shoot at 1/8 to 1/30 sec. with this high-speed film, and if you watch the traffic and shoot when it is stopped or slowed down, you can take a night scene with very little subject movement. Watch especially for the red double-decker buses that are so typical of London and include them in the background.

There is a handy railing and an iron pole right by the underground entrance that you can use to steady your camera. If you're athletic, you can stand up on the iron railing and get a very good higher view of the scene. Unfortunately, the STATUE OF EROS in the central island is not lighted, so the best thing to do is to silhouette it against the theater lights in the background.

Technique 2. Besides this "stop the traffic" technique, you can take longer exposures by using a slower color film, or stopping down your lens so that the moving cars will register as ribbons of colored light. The longer you leave the shutter open, the longer the ribbons of light will be. By stopping down to *f*/8 or even *f*/16, you can take exposures from 8 to 20 sec. on slow film, which will give you "rivers" of light.

Theaters. There are other night shots around Piccadilly Circus. Walk up SHAFTESBURY AVENUE and you'll be right in the middle of the glaring theater marquees. Your exposure will vary with the intensity of the light. If you are taking in only the bright lights, the exposure will be much less than if the marquee is only part of the scene. A good "guesstimate" on slow color film is an exposure of f/2 at 1/30 sec. for the lights; and on the general scene, use f/2 at ½ sec. On fast film, cut the exposure to f/2 at 1/125 sec. for lights, and f/2 at 1/30 sec. for the general scene.

As you walk around in this crowded area, you won't want to set up a tripod even if you have one, because it's a highly congested area. You can use light poles, sides of buildings, or even the tops of cars to support your camera.

3. The City of London

The "CITY" is about one square mile (approximately the size of Hyde Park) and lies along the north bank of the Thames, starting at FLEET STREET and ending at the TOWER OF LONDON. This is the first place you should go picture-hunting in London. In this relatively small area are some of the major sights, remnants of the past, and picturable details on buildings and monuments.

ENTRANCE TO THE CITY

The Royal Courts of Justice
The City entrance on Fleet Street has a number of good picture sights. One is the ROYAL COURTS OF JUSTICE, which can be taken from the traffic island facing them. Use the ornate iron lamp post by the underground entrance to frame the view on the right-hand side, and balance the turreted court buildings on the left. The foliage of overhanging trees can also be included to "hold in" the sky area. Watch the traffic in the street as you shoot. Wait until the red double-decker buses or the black London taxis are in your viewfinder before you shoot. These typical London vehicles add local color.

Try both vertical and horizontal framing and vary your lenses for different compositions. Include the policemen, who guard the crosswalk in front of the Courts. (The minimum height

The Royal Courts of Justice on Fleet Street look like a travel poster for London. Use the ornate iron lampposts as foreground interest for the overall scene.

Shop fronts along Fleet Street offer a chance for close-ups of typical London architecture. For best perspective, use a telephoto lens and shoot from across the street.

The Queen Victoria statue on Fleet Street is best photographed when the sun shines into the statue niche and illuminates detail. The griffin on top of the monument indicates that this is the boundary of the old City of London.

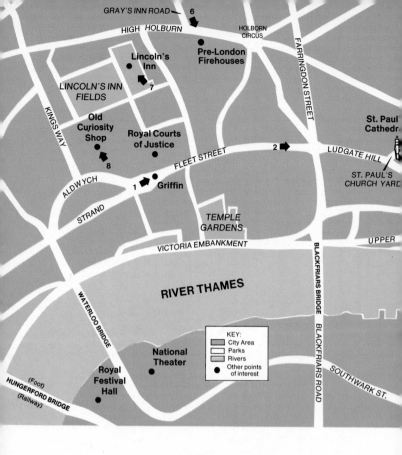

for a City of London Policeman is 5'10" and they are usually over 6' tall. This height plus their distinctive helmet makes them an identifying part of the "cityscape.")

The George

Across the street from the Royal Courts of Justice are several picturesque buildings. One is the GEORGE pub, which makes a colorful shot, with its black-painted woodwork, white stucco facade, and a displayed painting of King George.

Twining Tea Store

Almost across the street from the Royal Courts of Justice, look for the tiny facade and entrance to the TWINING TEA STORE. It has a sculptured lion over its doorway, flanked by white marble columns. Close by is the WIG AND PEN CLUB, its exterior covered by medallions showing the white wig and plumed pen trademarks of the legal profession.

Boundary Marker

The GRIFFIN-TOPPED MONUMENT in the center of the street identifies the boundary of the "OLD" CITY from new London. Include it in your shots of the general area for scene identification. A close-up of the monument also makes a good picture. On the sides there are statues of Queen Victoria and the Prince of Wales; and on top, the GRIFFIN symbol. The monument is very dark, so in order to show it clearly, be sure to choose a viewpoint where the statue is silhouetted against the sky or patterned in front of a light-colored building.

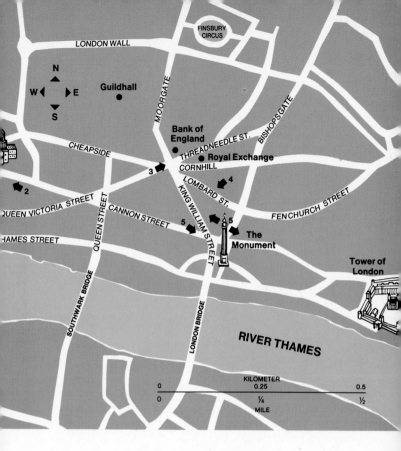

THE CITY OF LONDON

1. The entrance to the City on Fleet Street and views of the Royal Courts of Justice, the griffin/Queen Victoria/Prince of Wales Monument; the old pubs and prestige shops.

2. St. Paul's Cathedral—the long look up Ludgate Hill; the side views from St. Paul's Church Yard, plus the interior.

3. The Bank of England and the Royal Exchange up Threadneedle Street.

4. Old signs along Lombard Street.

5. The Monument, from where you can get some good views of downtown London and the Thames.

6. A group of pre-London fire houses, still standing.

7. Lincoln's Inn—old English-style buildings and grounds.

8. The still-standing Old Curiosity Shop, made famous by Dickens.

Other Sights

You can find more interesting bits of architecture as you walk about. These are easy pictures to take because the subjects themselves are eye catching. You don't need to "make" a picture; just line it up for a head-on shot and snap. The best lens to use is a telephoto, so you can shoot from across the street and get a good perspective, rather than tilting the camera for a close-up.

As you walk along Fleet Street looking through your telephoto lens for details, you may consider that in bygone days others were doing the same. Only then, the sport was to rent telescopes and focus on the dismembered heads of criminals displayed on spikes high overhead.

ST. PAUL'S CATHEDRAL

One of the best far-off views of ST. PAUL'S is from Fleet Street, just as it drops downhill and you're looking up to LUD-GATE HILL.

The Dome

Watch for a viewpoint along here, from which the black spire of ST. MARTIN'S is seemingly level with the top of ST. PAUL'S. It is said that Christopher Wren built ST. MARTIN'S so it would look as high as ST. PAUL'S. True or not, this phenomenon makes an interesting view. When shooting it, wait for the red double-decker buses to pile up in traffic below the blue railroad crossing overhead. With luck, you might also get a passing train.

A good close view of the Ludgate Hill side of St. Paul's can be taken from the traffic island in front. From there, you can include the STATUE OF QUEEN ANNE, as well as the overhead dome of the Cathedral. This will require a wide-angle lens; if you don't have one, back up farther and take in the same view with a normal lens.

Along the side of St. Paul's, where the buses park, you can get a different view. The best shot of the dome from this side is as you walk directly away from it on the walkway beside the park on ST. PAUL'S CHURCH YARD. You will notice that the dome seems to rise higher and higher as you walk away from it. For this reason, it's best to shoot with a telephoto lens so you can get a large image from a distance. Use vertical framing to take in the maximum height.

The flower-bordered parkway makes a good foreground for a color shot of the Cathedral. A wide-angle lens is useful here so that you can take in the foreground as well as the building in the back. Be sure to keep your camera vertical, otherwise you'll have an odd-shaped building that looks more like a pyramid than a church.

Inside

There are some good inside views of the CATHEDRAL. The first is the standard "right-against-the-front-door" picture, which you can take by pressing your camera overhead against the door and shooting straight up the center aisle.

48

From the top of Ludgate Hill, you can photograph this cluster of church towers, including the dome of St. Paul's Cathedral. Wait for the red buses to stop at the traffic light under the overhead railroad bridge, and include them in your view.

The Queen Anne Monument in front of St. Paul's can be photographed from the traffic island directly in front of the cathedral.

Flowers, in season, can add foreground color to an overall view of St. Paul's. Check your depth-of-field scale to be sure that the background building will be in sharp focus.

This abstract, made inside St. Paul's, is a multiple exposure of the choir lights thrown out of focus. See the text for how to take this unusual picture.

The Altar. The best interior view can be taken directly from the front of the choir stalls looking toward the altar. There is a convenient kneeling platform there, on which you can brace your camera. Use an aperture of *f*/4 for sufficient depth-of-field for both the choir in front and the altar in back. Our exposure for this one, on a dull day, was 1/15 sec. at *f*/4 on Agfachrome 64 daylight color film. But the exposure will vary with the brightness of the daylight outside. Be especially careful in metering this scene, because your meter will register the light from a large stained-glass window behind the altar, and the brightness of this area will affect your exposure reading. To compensate for this, aim your camera at the side and take a reading of the middle tones of the scene; then shift back and use the middle-tone reading to expose your original scene.

The Choir. You can have some fun with the small red-shaded choir lights by making a series of double and triple exposures that will give you an overall light pattern with the altar as background. To do this, expose only for the lights and move your camera enough so the lights don't overlap. Then make your final exposure of the altar. A typical shot could comprise a series of exposures at 1/60 sec. and *f*/4, and another of the altar at 1/30 sec. and *f*/4 on ASA 64 film. But you should bracket, since the effect will differ depending on the amount of exposure given.

The altar in St. Paul's makes an impressive color shot taken with the sunlight streaming down onto the gold book. This picture was taken from the back of the altar.

The Gold Book. There is a ready-made composition behind the altar, which you can walk around and shoot. This view includes the Gold Book containing World War II servicemen's names, which is displayed on a stand in back of the gold cross. If the light is right, you can get streams of daylight shining through the cross onto the opened book. Be sure to choose your viewpoint so that the light does not come directly into the lens but is shaded by the cross.

You can go to the top of the dome for some city views, which is worthwhile on a good clear day; but forget it if you're already footsore and the London fog creeps in.

THE BANK OF ENGLAND AND THE ROYAL EXCHANGE

A good view of the ROYAL EXCHANGE and the BANK OF ENGLAND is from the KING WILLIAM STREET side of the intersection that faces the MONUMENT TO THE DUKE OF WELLINGTON, looking up THREADNEEDLE STREET. This picture is best in the afternoon when the sun is shining on the front of the buildings and the statue. Again, watch for buses and taxis to lend color, and use the monument as a focal point.

Threadneedle Street is such a well-known landmark that it deserves some overall photos. Be sure to move back far enough to take in the Bank of England and the Royal Exchange.

LOMBARD STREET SIGNS

Just a short block from the Royal Exchange is a street of unusual signs — fanciful "logos" of the banks that do business there. A CAT AND FIDDLE, GRASSHOPPER, or an OWL are colorful reminders of the days when pictures were used instead of lettering to help illiterates find the right address.

You can "pull up" the individual signs on LOMBARD STREET with a telephoto lens, or "stack" them up one in back of the other. If you try a composition of a number of signs, be sure

53

Overhead signs should be photographed from a distance with a telephoto lens so that there is better perspective on the vertical panel. This cat-and-the-fiddle on Lombard Street was taken with a 105 mm lens.

to stop down and focus about one-third the distance into the scene so that *all* the emblems will be sharp. With a telephoto lens, you should stop down all the way and use a compensatingly slow shutter speed. When you do this, be sure to brace your camera against a light pole or the side of a building so that it will be steady.

The best light on the signs is from about noon to 3 P.M.; at other times, the street is in shadow, and the signs are not as colorful.

Lombard Street signs are fun to photograph. A moderate telephoto, like a 105 mm, is ideal for pulling them closer when shooting from street level. The light for these shots is best around noon.

*The Monument to the Great
Fire of London can be
climbed to the top for city
views. To minimize distortion
caused by pointing the camera upward to photograph the
monument itself, be sure to
turn the camera to the vertical.*

MONUMENT

One of the best overlooks of London is from the 202-foot-high **MONUMENT** to the great fire of London, which was erected in 1677. You can climb up the 311 steps and take photos from the viewing platform on top. The view is not spectacular, but there are two good overall views.

One is looking northwest to the **FINANCIAL CENTER**, and the other is looking down the Thames toward the **TOWER OF LONDON** and **TOWER BRIDGE**.

These views are best on a sunny day in the afternoon. Be sure to take a polarizing filter with you, if you have one, to sharpen the detail. A skylight filter as well as slight underexposure (one-half stop down from your meter reading will do) can also help to gain contrast.

Watch in particular for river traffic. At times, large ships pass by and the **TOWER BRIDGE** is opened up. A long lens will help enlarge this view for an unusual shot.

PRE-FIRE-OF-LONDON HOUSES

There are a few old houses still left from before the big seventeenth-century blaze. These dwellings are squeezed in along **HIGH HOLBORN** between modern buildings. They may look like a "put on," but they are the real thing. You can take a picture to show them from the intersection of **HIGH HOLBORN** and **GRAY'S INN ROAD**. The best time is in the late afternoon.

Although this is a straight-on shot, you can vary it by using the griffin-topped monument in the foreground and only parts of the houses in the back. A wide-angle is the most effective lens for this treatment.

Amid modern structures stands this group of old buildings that survived the Great Fire of London in 1666. Choose a sunny day to bring out the detail of the half-timbered fronts.

This is a classic view of Lincoln's Inn, taken from the inside the gardens. Frame this scene with tree foliage for added depth.

LINCOLN'S INN

A residential hostelry for young lawyers, **LINCOLN'S INN** dates back to the fifteenth century. You can enter the grounds through a gateway and capture the grace and charm of warm-colored red brick buildings surrounded by flowers, trees, and lawns. This is a scene made for color photography.

The best time to go is around noon when the grounds are open to the public. Besides the main buildings, there is a

The interior of the library at Lincoln's Inn offers another opportunity to photograph a scene that has not changed for centuries. This view from the overhead balcony was taken on ASA 64 film at 1 sec. at f/4. The camera was braced against the iron railing.

The shadows cast by the intricate, wrought-iron park entrance inside the Lincoln's Inn grounds, makes a strong backlighted pattern. Look for varying angles of light to add interest to your pictures.

The imposing entrance gate to the walled Lincoln's Inn law students' residence is a fine example of the diversity of London's architecture.

square that is entered through an ornate iron gateway. This too makes a good shot, backlighted against the soft green of the square.

Outside of the inn there is a large square called **LINCOLN'S INN FIELDS**, where the law students, lawyers, and other people congregate during lunchtime. Some unwrap their sandwiches and eat under huge oak trees, others play tennis, and some just stroll around the grounds. All this activity makes for good candid camera shots. You too can relax under the trees and pick off the action with a telephoto lens.

Dickens's "Old Curiosity Shop" can be photographed from the front to show over-all detail, or from the side to accent the askew roof line.

THE OLD CURIOSITY SHOP

Just off **LINCOLN'S INN FIELDS** is, what is said to be, the oldest standing house in London, the **OLD CURIOSITY SHOP**. You can take some good views of the outside as well as the interior.

A head-on view can be taken from directly across the street facing the front, but a more interesting angle is from the alleyway across from the corner. From this angle, the irregularities of the old roof become photographically more evident. If you just want to picture the house alone, you will need patience; all the tours stop there, producing a constant stream of visitors.

The interior is best taken with flash, because the light is very low. You should ask the owner's permission for this.

You will find many more sights to picture in the area of the **CITY OF LONDON**. Some of the outstanding pictorial sights are suggested here, but if you have the time, explore the area with the help of a good guide book (we recommend *Michelin*) and find additional pictures.

4. Kensington-Knightsbridge Commerce and Culture Sights

The area south of Hyde Park and Kensington Gardens is a mixture of former Victorian splendor, reconstructed houses, and funky shopping streets. These subjects provide a feast for your camera lens and capture a part of London where culture and commerce live side by side.

THE ALBERT MEMORIAL

This monument, which stands in Kensington Gardens opposite the Royal Albert Hall, is a Victorian masterpiece, and as such, it makes a great camera subject. It is out in the open and can be pictured from many angles, but the best is from the front with a view of **PRINCE ALBERT** facing you through the archway. Since the entire structure is 175 feet high and sits atop a flight of granite steps, it's necessary to photograph it at a distance to avoid distortion.

The best place to take the overall views is from the entry walkway of the park. A normal lens will just about take in the entire scene from there, and a medium telephoto (80 to 105 mm) will bring the central spire up close. Try some compositions with the tree foliage covering part of the sky; and if you have a variety of lenses, move closer or farther back and try for various effects. (You'll notice that the monument seems to change height with the distance.)

The best view of the Albert Memorial is from directly in front when the sun shines on it from a side angle. This lighting will give a partial silhouette of the statue of Prince Albert, while bringing out the detail of the carved pedestal.

KEY:
City Area
Parks
Rivers
● Other points
of interest
◉ Fountains

QUEENSWAY

BAYSWATER ROAD

THE RING

KENSINGTON PALACE GARDENS

KENSINGTON GARDENS

Kensington Palace

ROUND POND

KENSINGTON PALACE GREEN

10

Restaurant

11

Serpentine Gallery

12

Albert Memorial

1

KENSINGTON ROAD

Royal College of Organists

Royal Albert Hall

2

GLOUCESTER ROAD

QUEENS GATE

EXHIBITION ROAD

Victoria & Albert Museum

Science Museum ●

Natural History Museum

3

CROMWELL ROAD

KENSINGTON—KNIGHTSBRIDGE COMMERCE AND CULTURE SITES AND HYDE PARK VIEWS AND MONUMENTS

1. The Albert Memorial "wedding cake," which has 197 pieces of "icing-like" sculpture.

 2. Royal College of Organists—another decorative structure that makes an interesting picture.

 3. Natural History Museum—a "whale of a building" that actually exhibits whales.

 4. Victoria and Albert Museum where the Raphael cartoons are on exhibit.

5. Brompton Square—Georgian houses set around a central park.

 6. Beauchamp Place—a colorful shopping street.

 7. Harrod's—the world famous department store which is worth some shots.

 8. Marble Arch—views by day or night.

9. Speakers' Corner—a place for characters and candids.

 10. The Serpentine—a classic view of the towers of Parliament and Westminster Abbey.

 11. The restaurant area is ideal for pictures of kids, lake activity, and diners "alfresco."

 12. A look in on the Serpentine Gallery, and a look out on Henry Moore sculptures.

 13. Several ways to shoot the Wellington Arch, plus other details.

Since the sky forms the background, the use of filters will dramatize the scene. Use a polarizing filter to darken the sky, or a skylight filter to cut down the excess blue (this also helps to warm up the colors on the monument).

Sunlight really makes the monument glow on color film, so if the sun is playing "hide and go seek" on that day, be patient and wait for it to come out. The best time of day is around noon when the sun strikes the Albert statue, although a sidelight later in the afternoon or early in the morning can also be effective.

Besides the distant shots, you should also try some close-ups of the frieze figures. With a wide-angle lens, you can focus on the detail; and by aiming your camera straight up, you can capture the spire as well. (Use the depth-of-field focusing techniques described in the "Tips and Techniques" section.)

ROYAL COLLEGE OF ORGANISTS

This is a "drive by" picture that is located inside the ring road around the ROYAL ALBERT HALL across from the Albert Memorial. As with the monument, this building is also a bit of Victorian whimsy. But in this case the theme is baroque, with cream-colored trim and musical instruments decorating the chocolate brown facade.

The best light is around noon when the ornate front isn't shaded by the huge Albert Hall rotunda. An overall view or a close-up for detail would be equally effective.

NATURAL HISTORY MUSEUM

This enormous structure looks like a medieval castle on the outside. The main entry hall inside is as large as a railway terminal. You can easily spend a day wandering through and taking pictures.

This interior shot of the whale exhibit inside the Natural History Museum is easy to take. Use a wide-angle lens and shoot from the balcony surrounding the display.

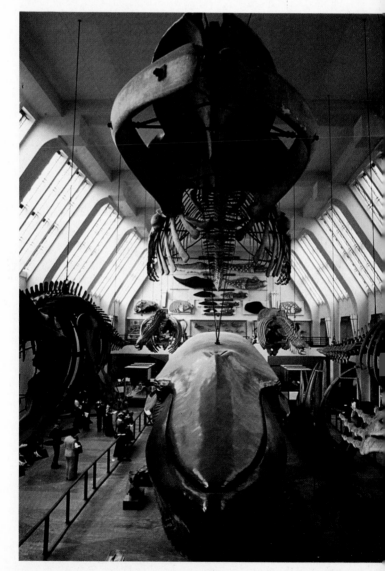

The Inside

The hall can be taken just as you enter. There is a convenient display stand by the doorway which you can use to brace your camera for the necessarily long exposure. A wide-angle lens will take in the entire scene. To focus for this and other large indoor areas with a wide-angle lens, set the far-distance infinity mark just within the depth-of-field marking for the f-stop that you're using, and the entire scene will be sharp. (This system is much better than trying to focus accurately in dim light on the small detail that a wide-angle lens shows.)

The Whale Hall. A highlight of the museum is the WHALE HALL, in which a 91-foot-long blue whale is displayed. A convenient balcony running around the upper half of the room gives a good vantage point for photography. You can walk around and choose a view, but be sure to look at the whale head-on. At this angle, you can take in the entire whale, as well as the tiny people looking at it from below. A wide-angle lens is necessary to take in the view. (We used a 24 mm, which seemed just right.)

The exposure for this shot is about $f/4$ at 1/15 sec. on ASA 64 daylight color film. With ASA 400 film, your shutter speed can be increased to 1/60 sec. with your aperture ½ stop smaller—between $f/4$ and $f/5.6$.

The Children's Section. Another fun picture area is the CHILDREN'S SECTION where giant, colorful, mock figures explain the functions of the human body. This area is spotlighted, so you need a high-speed indoor film, such as Ektachrome 160 film (tungsten). With this fast film, you can shoot handholdable exposures of about 1/30 sec. at $f/4$. (An aperture of $f/4$ is favorable for these indoor scenes because at this slightly stopped-down lens opening, you can shoot with a fast enough shutter speed to stop camera and subject motion and still have enough depth of focus to get the needed sharpness.)

When shooting candids in this area, as well as in others, wait until your subject is in the right position of natural action before pressing the shutter release. You should also look over the field of possible subjects and choose the most colorful or attractive one to be your center of interest.

Besides the inside shooting and the views outside during the day, the entire building is illuminated at night, offering another kind of picture.

At Night

The night shot can be taken by using the iron fence as support for your camera. Simply hold it against the vertical rods for an upright view, or lay it on the horizontal sections for a straight-across composition. Use high-speed daylight film for the night shots and bracket your exposures. Starting with 1 sec. at $f/2.8$, double the time on the "B" (bulb) setting (just count out the seconds as "one-thousand-and-one," "one-thousand-and-two," etc.) and continue up to 2, 4, and 8 sec.

You will have to look for openings in the tree foliage where you can take in the front entrance through the fence.

VICTORIA AND ALBERT MUSEUM

The Raphael Tapestry Cartoons

One of the main features at the VICTORIA AND ALBERT MUSEUM is the collection of original tapestry cartoons by RAPHAEL. These priceless drawings are displayed in a gallery that is dimly lighted by high overhead windows. For photography an added complication to the poor light is that the drawings are covered by glass that is full of reflections. Part of the reflections can be eliminated with a polarizing filter, but not all of them. The best method is to choose a position off center and look through the polarizing filter, while rotating it, to observe at what angle the glass is free from glare. You will have to walk around and try various positions until you find the best view.

Good color shots of the paintings inside the Victoria and Albert Museum can be taken with Ektachrome indoor film. Exposure on this spotlighted altarpiece was 1/30 sec. at f/2.8.

On your museum visits, look for works of art that typify the country you are visiting. An example is this painting of St. George, the patron saint of England, in the Victoria and Albert Museum.

We found that the average exposure was *f*/4 (which was needed to sharpen up the side view of the cartoons) at 1 sec. with ASA 64 daylight color film. The full-second shutter speed was for the adjusted 2.5 filter factor of the polarizing filter. A better method is to use Ektachrome 400 film (daylight) and shorten the exposure to 1/4–1/8 sec. at *f*/4. The ASA 64 film is preferable, however, because it is finer grained and therefore has better resolution on the details of the drawings.

Other Objects
There are many other art objects to picture in the museum. A huge **ALTAR PIECE** with scenes from the life of **ST. GEORGE** struck our fancy. This medieval painting of the Spanish school is displayed in a spotlighted area where there is an information board stand that makes a handy substitute tripod. By holding the camera against the edge, or against the board itself, you can make exposures up to 1 sec.

We tried both daylight and tungsten color film on this subject and found that Ektachrome 160 film (tungsten) was far superior in color to the daylight film which turned an off-color red. When in doubt as to the proportion of daylight to indoor light, you can make the same kind of experiment to make sure you have a variety of results.

By the way, here's a suggestion for camera note-taking: When you would like to record information about a subject or sight, and you don't want to bother copying it all down, all you have to do is take an exposure of the explanation or description (if there is one) on the frame following the subject. This way you will get both subject and info on the same roll of film, and you can even project them both during your slide shows.

BROMPTON SQUARE

There is a small hidden street of Georgian Houses almost next door to the Victoria and Albert Museum on the Brompton Road. The old houses—built like modern attached townhouses

To capture the park-like setting of Brompton Square,
photograph the charming
Georgian buildings through
the foliage of the trees.

A normal lens can be used
to photograph the front
doorways and iron railings
of the Brompton Square
houses.

— are set around a U-shaped turnoff called Brompton Square that enters this country-looking area and turns back to the main road.

To capture the park-like setting, photograph the buildings through the foliage of the trees and include part of the garden. A wide-angle lens will take in both the houses and the park in the center. You can also walk around with a normal lens and shoot front doorways in the enclosed iron-fenced yards.

BEAUCHAMP PLACE

Beauchamp Place is an expensive but delightfully funky street of small shops, restaurants, and pubs.

Almost anything can happen there. A small sports car might be parked with two lordly Afghan hounds peering out and surveying the scene, style-conscious girls may click by on the sidewalk, or you may see an artsy looking character slouched against a doorway.

The shop windows are ideal for close-ups. There are displays of silverware, dolls, antiques, and lots of trendy clothes.

A pair of elegant Afghan hounds await the return of their owner from a shopping trip in stylish Beauchamp Place.

Beauchamp Place is lined with small, picturesque shops. Keep your camera preset and prefocused to be ready for whatever catches your interest.

Shop windows make interesting photos. Choose the ones that are well lighted and on the sunny side of the street. If there are reflections, shoot from an angle rather than straight-on, or try a polarizing filter.

71

A good shooting technique is to combine the window displays with the passing window-watchers. Move in close to a window display with a wide-angle lens and include the sidewalk in half of the viewfinder frame. When the right subject walks toward you, click . . . and you'll have both. It's a little sneaky, but it works. For this shot, prefocus on the window display and use your depth-of-field scale to set the focus so that the passing subject will be sharp as well. (Check "Tips and Techniques" for more on the depth-of-field scale.)

Exposure can be a problem in this situation, because the light on the window will be much less than the light on the street. The best technique is to split the difference; that is, take one reading of the display, and another of the street scene; then choose a setting between the two extremes. Another way to handle this problem is to choose a scene where the sun shines in the window but backlights the oncoming subject. In this case the exposure will be nearly equal for both.

Street scenes can also be interesting. For some of these, include the white church tower at the end of the street for a Montmarte look that says Utrillo was here. This treatment calls for a normal lens, or even a moderate telephoto to condense the storefronts for a tighter composition. In such scenes, focus about one-third the distance into the picture for maximum sharpness.

A telephoto lens is a must for candid pictures. Find a convenient doorway where you can blend into the background and watch the passersby. Prefocus on a crack in the pavement or a meter post that they will have to pass; then shoot when they step on the target. You may see someone that will make a good close-up. In this case nothing works as well as asking the sub- ect, in a polite way, to allow you to make a close-up portrait of him or her.

HARROD'S

This turn-of-the-century building with its turrets, towers, and awnings looks so impressive that at first one thinks it's another great museum or a public building. It's not, but in it's own way, **HARROD'S** is as much a part of the London scene as the big cultural sights, for this is the store where you can buy a needle or an elephant. It's worth a look inside as well as out.

The outside view is easy to take because **BROMPTON ROAD** is very wide and you can stand on the opposite side to include the structure. The only trick is to find the right distance so that you can take it all in without having to tilt your camera and distort the vertical lines. Close-up views of some of the window displays can be interesting, as there are usually some exotic items shown.

The chauffers' parking entrance on the side is a good place to watch for a candid of someone entering a Rolls or a

All around Harrod's, chauf-
fered cars wait for the shoppers. The gleaming radiators
of these elegant cars make for
good foreground interest and
tell something about the
store's clientele.

Harrod's is easy to photograph from the outside,
from the opposite side of
Brompton Road. Try to find
the right distance so the
verticals will not be dis-
torted by camera tilt.

Bentley parked there. And around the corner, there is an overwhelming number of expensive cars waiting for returning shoppers. A long lens is good for capturing these subjects just as they enter the cars. But watch out for the liveried man who may take you for a *Paparazzi* and challenge your right to shoot.

5. Hyde Park

The park is enormous and on a brief London visit you won't have time to explore all of it. But there are some easy-to-reach locations that capture the atmosphere of this "middle of the city" green breathing space. You can easily drive to these sights, along the eastern edge of the park and down through the middle over the **SERPENTINE** lake.

The best time for a tour of the park is on a weekend when the Londoners crowd the green meadows to play, row, and even swim in the lake (during the tourist season, there are many visitors on weekdays as well).

MARBLE ARCH

A good view of **MARBLE ARCH** can be taken to the right of **CUMBERLAND GATE**, where **PARK LANE** turns onto **BAYSWATER ROAD** at the northeast corner of **HYDE PARK**. The traffic there is very heavy, but you can pull off to the side, or ask your cab to do

Slanting frontlight brings out the detail in this view of Marble Arch. Because light is so important to the effectiveness of such scenes, try to photograph them only when the light is right.

so, while you make some quick exposures of the arch. The best light is in the morning when the front of the arch is in sunlight.

For a more interesting view, cross the street and shoot from the park in front of the arch. From there you have a number of pictorial possibilities. One is to frame the structure with the flags that line the approach — a slightly off-side angle is better than a head-on — but move to a position where the flags are not covering the arch. Another view is to use the planted flowers for foreground color. By turning the camera vertically, you can include the foreground and still keep the vertical lines of the arch straight.

MARBLE ARCH is also lighted at night, and you can take the same views then with the camera either on a tripod or supported against a pole. (Look for more on night illumination in the "Tips and Techniques" section.)

SPEAKERS' CORNER

One "people" activity that you can only photograph on the week-end is the crowds gathered at SPEAKERS' CORNER opposite MARBLE ARCH. You can have some fun there shooting news-type pictures of the orators and their audience.

WELLINGTON ARCH

The best light on WELLINGTON ARCH (located at Hyde Park Corner) is in the afternoon toward sunset. A sunset sky can reflect a gold color onto the arch and statuary on top that makes it look like it was made of the precious metal.

A straight-on view of the Wellington Arch should be taken from a distance with a tele- *photo lens. This makes the figures on top appear particularly impressive.*

Wellington's statue is best photographed from the side so that the equestrian figure stands out in silhouette against the sky.

Besides the straight-on view, you can include the **MONU-MENT TO THE DUKE OF WELLINGTON** in the foreground. This can be best done with a wide-angle lens, but a normal lens can also be used. You can frame this shot by moving back under the trees and composing the foliage around the monument and the arch.

This view also can be taken at night when it is illuminated. Use the same techniques recommended for **MARBLE ARCH**.

The iron gate of the arch has added picture possibilities: Move in close and use the round **WELLINGTON SHIELD** as a center for an interesting round composition.

THE SERPENTINE OVERLOOK

A picturesque scene that will have your viewers asking, "Where did you take it?" is a shot looking over the **SERPENTINE** from the bridge. The view of the distant towers of Parliament and Westminster Abbey, with the lake and the park in the foreground, looks like a country scene, not one in the middle of a large city. The trick to this shot is that you must have a telephoto lens of at least 135 mm, or better still, a 200 mm, and you need a clear day.

The best time is in the afternoon when the sun lights up the distant buildings. Include some of the boats on the lake for foreground interest and use a skylight filter or even a polarizer to cut the haze.

There are other shots you can take from this bridge: "parkscapes" with strollers, and close-ups of boaters on the water. Just over the bridge is a modern restaurant that is picturable, as well as being a good spot for a snack. There is also a children's playground in the area that makes for good candids.

Further on, the **SERPENTINE GALLERY** and the **HENRY MOORE SCULPTURES** offer other picture opportunities. The

The modern restaurant just off the Serpentine in Hyde Park is one of the few examples of recent architecture that you can photograph around London.

The Henry Moore statues in Hyde Park offer a chance for some interesting photos. Kids clambering on and around these large forms add liveliness to the scene.

giant, free-form pieces are out in the open and you can walk about looking for angles. One possibility is to wait for one of the many children's groups that suddenly descend from buses and clamber over the sculptures; or you can relate the sculptures to the fields and trees beyond by moving in close and framing the view through them. There is one huge piece that is reminiscent of tree trunks. A shot through the sculpture of the lines of trees behind it effectively interprets the sculptor's intent in making the piece part of the scene.

6. London Miscellany

SHOPS AND STREET MARKETS

You can photograph some of the many street markets that take place throughout the city; some of them are in SOHO, but the most well known is the SATURDAY MARKET ON PORTOBELLO ROAD IN KENSINGTON.

At these outdoor "bazaars," you may even run across some recent arrivals from Britain's former Far East colonies, or visitors from the Arab states. It's quite a startling sight to see the covered faces of Moslem women as they circulate among the people of London.

Another outdoor sight is the fruit and vegetable carts that are often parked on the sidewalk in front of the major stores. They are not only colorful in themselves, but they add color to what might otherwise be a drab, treeless city street.

Window-shopping is also good for picture-shopping. There are many speciality stores throughout the city that sell silver, snuff, china, and other typically British products. Close-ups of these "windows into the London scene" make good souvenir shots.

A good overall view of street markets can be taken from the balconies of surrounding buildings.

Look for bright splashes of color in the market scene. Here, the oriental rugs laid right on the city street are a vivid contrast to the usual gray of London.

The concentration of shops inside the **BURLINGTON ARCADE** make particularly good pictures, both as individual stores and collectively. The **ARCADE** is right on **PICCADILLY**, near **BOND STREET**. There is plenty of skylight to shoot by, and many typical products are displayed. It's a good place to capture the flavor of old London, including the **BELL RINGER** who sounds the closing of the Arcade at the end of the day.

Street markets, often looking like oriental bazaars, are held on certain days. The traffic is blocked off and you can wander around with your camera seeking out the colorful and the unusual.

You don't have to make a special trip for these shopping pictures (except for the **BURLINGTON ARCADE** and the famed **PORTOBELLO ROAD OUTDOOR MARKET**), but if you are shopping and have your camera with you, you may find a "picture" bargain that is as good as an actual purchase.

PUBS! PUBS! PUBS!

London is **PUB** country; even the *Michelin London* guide lists an alphabetical row of famed watering places. These pubs are geat subjects for your camera. The exteriors of the old ones look like restored museum pieces, and the characteristic signs

Old-fashioned signs can be found above the pubs and stores in the City of London. Look up as you walk around, and pick these off with a long-focal-length lens.

Many London pubs have pre-served their old façades. Crosslight helps bring out their detailed decorations.

with paintings of kings and nobles, and birds and beasts, make a series of historic close-ups.

Several favorites are the **GEORGE**, at the entrance to the City on Fleet Street; the **CLARENCE**, on **WHITEHALL**; and the **DUKE OF YORK**, on **VICTORIA STREET**. All three of these pubs make interesting pictures and are good refreshment stops. But you'll surely discover some of your own in your meanderings about the city. When you do, remember that they too are a part of the London scene, and take some shots.

MEWS AND MORE

London is an old city with many details left over from times past, so look for the small characteristic shots as well as the big sights while traveling around the city.

Often a chance encounter makes a better picture than a major sight that you set out to photograph. In London, some of the interesting details to watch for are the **MEWS**, or alleyways, between the major streets. These "off street" areas are where many of the more arty and eccentric people live. You may see a typical British sports car parked under a window full of flowering plants, or even a bicycle propped against a studio wall. The English have a talent for making their yards, windows, and entrances homey-looking with climbing roses, picket fences, and sculptured door knockers. Some of these scenes will add a contrast of "village-looking" shots to your city pictures.

Other details to watch for are the **POST BOXES**; the **BOBBIES**; **BOUNDARY MARKERS**; remnants of the old city walls; **IRON LAMP POSTS** sculptured with dolphins and lions; and even **OLD IRON HOLDERS** that were used to hold flaming torches.

The mews of London afford
many charming shots.
Look up and down these narrow side streets for picture
possibilities.

BOAT TRIPS ON THE THAMES

The boats leave from the foot of **WESTMINSTER BRIDGE**,
but, except for the immediate area around the bridge, there's
not much to picture until you reach **GREENWICH**. The **BANKS OF
THE THAMES** are covered with commercial docks and the backs
of nondescript buildings with only a peek here and there of what
lies beyond.

SHOOTING IN WET WEATHER

This section is included here because like it or not, in
London you might be faced with the problem of what and how
to photograph when it's gray and rainy, or gray and foggy out-
doors.

The first thing to do is to keep some high-speed color or
black-and-white film handy. You should carry several rolls with
you at all times because you can use them for interiors as well
as for low-light outdoor shooting.

Outdoors

City street scenes acquire a new look in wet weather. The
sidewalk and street pavements become giant mirrors reflecting
passing pedestrians, cars, and window displays. Often lights

84

are turned on, which add bright color accents to the gray scene. Umbrellas are unfurled and bright-colored raingear is worn. A look down from an overhead window on a pattern of colorful umbrellas against the glistening pavements can make an effective shot.

Textures of brick, wood, stone, and marble become more apparent because the moisture brings out the color. Tree leaves glisten and the grass looks greener. A window plant, over-looked on sunny days because of competing sights, suddenly seems jewel-bright in a gray setting.

The parks become a Japanese-print two-dimensional world. All you see is the foreground and a hazy outline in back. Look along the edges of the lakes or pools for swimming ducks, swans, or boats; picture them against the outlined background. Statues also become more lifelike and intimate, because they are closed off from the competing world around them by the fog and rain.

Wet weather is the time for close-ups of flowers and portraits of people. The soft, hazy light gives a bounced-light effect without glaring highlights or harsh shadows. This is the time to take those vivid, full color saturation pictures in which the colors seem to glow.

You don't need special equipment to photograph in wet weather except an umbrella. For cover, nothing works as well as an umbrella. Not only does it keep the equipment dry, but it keeps the raindrops far enough away from the lens so they don't blur the image with streaks of gray.

One of the best views on the riverboat tour is of the Houses of Parliament over the Thames. Even on a foggy day, *when only the outlines of the buildings are visible, this view is highly effective and entirely typical of London.*

Indoors

An alternate to outdoor wet-weather shooting is to visit one of the many museums and take pictures inside. Unfortunately, some of them, like the TATE GALLERY and the NATIONAL GALLERY, do not permit photography. But others do, and our favorite is the BRITISH MUSEUM.

THE BRITISH MUSEUM

There are endless subjects to photograph in the BRITISH MUSEUM on a rainy day, or on any day.

Statuary in the British Museum is well lighted for photography. Use indoor color film (tungsten) for the best tone on the marble figures.

Move in close on small museum subjects so that the detail will show up clearly. (Close-ups can be taken with a macro lens or any other lens that focuses in to 18 inches.)

The Elgin Marbles

A particularly good section for photography is the GREEK ARCHEOLOGY SECTION where the ELGIN MARBLES are displayed, along with excellent examples from other expeditions. The illumination is from spotlights, so it doesn't matter what the day is like outside. You should use a high-speed tungsten color film, or a conversion filter to change the daylight film to tungsten. The lighting is good enough for handheld exposures on high-speed film; but when possible, steady the camera against a nearby doorway, pillar, or stand. (Our exposures ran from 1/15 to 1/30 sec. at f/2.8 on Ektachrome 160 film (tungsten).)

The Medieval Galleries

Another interesting section in the BRITISH MUSEUM is the MEDIEVAL GALLERIES, where there are opportunities for close-ups of rare pieces.

THEATER PHOTOGRAPHY

Officially you can't take photos of a theater production, and usually this prohibition is clearly posted. There are many good reasons for this, chiefly the nuisance of clicking cameras and flashing lights during the performance. There are also union and trade regulations, as well as trademark restrictions. In short, it's simpler all around just to say "no."

These restrictions don't mean that it's never possible to take pictures. They can be taken inconspicuously without even raising the camera to your eye. We have photographed some performances—some with permission and some without—and no one knew that the pictures were being taken. We don't advise you to do this, but perhaps you can convince the management to give you a chance shot.

If you should have this opportunity, the best time to shoot is after the performance during the curtain calls. Since most good plays have several bows, you will have a chance to shoot. In order to take such a shot with a minimum of fuss, preset your camera for focus and exposure, and use a high-speed indoor film. Preset for focus by using the depth-of-field-scale setting. Place the infinity mark just inside the depth-of-field scale for the aperture you will use. With a wide-angle lens set at f/4, your image will be sharp from about 12 feet to infinity, and with a normal 50 mm lens, from 25 feet to infinity. By setting your focus with the depth-of-field scale, your image will be sharp at a distance of 30 feet to infinity. All you have to do is raise the camera to your eye and shoot. The sound of the applause will cover the sound of the shutter release.

One thing you don't want to do is have the picture reproduced, unless you get permission; but you will be able to project it for your friends and put it in your scrapbook.

7. Hampton Court

Although outside of London, **HAMPTON COURT** is well worth the extra trip. There are 50 acres of gardens surrounding a vast medieval palace—both very picturable.

The Grounds

The entrance to the grounds is through the **LION GATES**, right off **HAMPTON COURT ROAD**. The gates themselves make a good shot as you enter. At the south end of the park, turn left and go through a gateway to the formal gardens. This is where you'll have a chance for many views.

The Great Fountain. Walk around the outer circular walkway from where you can take a view through the **GREAT FOUNTAIN** of the Palace beyond.

Closer in to the fountain, you can use the water lilies as foreground color. Move in and choose the best clusters of flowers for the close-up. In order to have the Palace in the background sharp, as well as the water lilies in the foreground, stop your lens down and use the depth-of-field markings to set your focus. (Check the "Tips and Techniques" section for information on the depth-of-field scale.)

In the opposite direction, across the canal, is a body of water called the **LONG WATER**, which makes a good scenic country-like view, with white ducks swimming about.

Lily pads in the fountains behind Hampton Court make a good foreground for overall views of the gardens. Here, focus on the foreground and let the background soften for a pictorial effect.

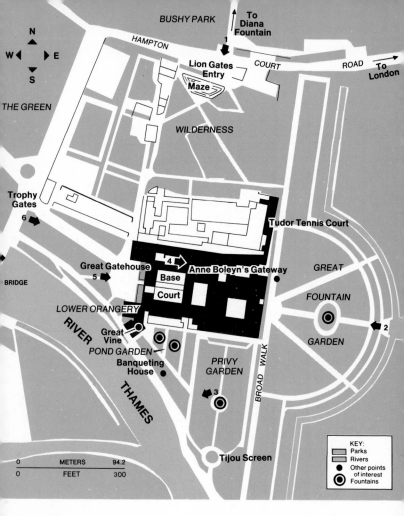

HAMPTON COURT AND ITS GARDENS

 1. The lion gates entry angles.

 2. In and around the great fountain garden—views far, near, and very close.

 3. The "insider's" inside garden picture postcard view.

 4. The Palace.

 5. The main entry views of medieval stone animals against the battlements.

 6. The long view down the trophy gates entry.

 7. A classic Gainsborough-style view of the Thames River and the court grounds.

90

The side garden at Hampton
Court offers a charming view
of a typical "English garden."
Compose this shot so that the
palace building will show in
the background.

The Formal Gardens. If you are at HAMPTON COURT in
the morning, the sun will shine on the back of the palace where
the formal gardens are located. You can look for reflections in
the pool by squatting down and finding a low camera angle. An
interesting composition to shoot is the reflection among the
water lilies. Again, be sure to stop down for this picture, just as
you did for the one with the fountain in front and the Palace in
back. Because the water reflection is like a mirror, you have to
focus on the image where the Palace is reflected, as well as the
surface on which the water lilies float.

The main entry to Hampton Court makes a good head-on shot from the open courtyard in front. Because the courtyard is so large, you can move back as far as necessary to take in the whole building with any lens.

The Privy Garden. A stroll down the broad walk to the south takes you into the PRIVY GARDEN, where there are some good picture-postcard views. An especially good shot is looking toward the THAMES away from the main Palace toward the BANQUETING HOUSE on the river bank. To make the scene as colorful as possible, look for the brightest masses of flowers, and move in close so that they fill the foreground. Again, use the stopped-down depth-of-field-scale technique to ensure sharpness.

These flower gardens not only make good general views, but also excellent close-ups. For the close-up photographs, move in as near as your lens will focus, or use a telephoto lens to bring the flowers closer. Watch the play of light on the flowers: A strong sidelight, or even a backlight, will give you higher color saturation than a frontlight; a dark background, such as an area of shade, will also accent the bright flower colors. If you choose a dark background, be sure to take a very close-up meter reading of the flowers, or just stop down one-half stop from the indicated exposure. This will ensure that the flower coloring won't be over-exposed because of the influence of the dark background; and the underexposure will turn the dark background even blacker.

The Main Entrance. After the garden shots, walk around the Palace to the main entrance on the other side. This offers a contrast to the formal garden views. It looks more like Disneyland, with towers, twisted chimneys, and a bridge over a moat that is guarded by heraldic animals carved in stone.

You can have some fun picturing these outlandish sculptures with a wide-angle lens. By moving in close, you can frame the view so that the lion, the falcon, or the unicorn appears to be over the walls guarding the castle or soaring over the top of the crenellated towers. Use the depth-of-field-scale technique here.

There are two lines of statues, one on each side of the entry. Choose the side that is in front sunlight for your close-ups. Move your camera viewpoint down, up, and around until you have the framing you want. Keep in mind that the background is also important, so be sure to line up the foreground pieces against the part of the tower, gate, or walls that you want to show.

A variation of this close-up wide-angle technique is to back off and use a telephoto lens to condense the line of sculptures. A moderate telephoto of 80 to 135 mm is sufficient to

A poster-like picture can be taken of the front gate of Hampton Court framed by stone animal statues. For the most sharpness use the depth-of-field focusing technique described in the "Tips and Techniques" section.

"stack" them up and keep the entire line in focus; but you will have to stop down for the needed depth. You can determine how far to stop down by pressing your depth-of-field preview button, so you can see the scene at the "taking," not the "viewing," aperture.

Outside the Moat. There are other views to consider besides the animal parade at the entrance. Look at the angles from the outside of the MOAT; from there you can really capture the feeling of a medieval castle by showing the deep ditch in front and the entry gate, the walls, and the towers in back. Watch the direction of light and shoot from the side where you get a cross light that shows texture and detail.

Farther back, on the roadway that leads to the TROPHY GATES, there are opportunities for overall shots. The view depends on your lens, but you will notice that the farther you back away, the higher the towers and chimneys seem to be. So if you want a more dramatic picture, take it from a greater distance with a telephoto lens.

A skylight filter, or even a polarizer, will add contrast to your scene by darkening the sky. If you don't have these filters, a one-half stop underexposure will also help.

As you go out by the TROPHY GATES, turn left and continue on the bridge over the THAMES. From about midway, you can take an overall view of the Palace, the grounds, and the river in the foreground. Your picture will look like a Gainsborough landscape. Watch the river boat activity and shoot when one of the sightseeing steamers leaves the dock in front of the Palace grounds.

An eighteenth-century painter's view of Hampton Court was photographed from the bridge that crosses the Thames. Wait for the tourist boats and include them in the scene.

The Interior

Photography is not permitted inside the Palace. When we asked why not, the guard replied that Hampton Court is royal property, and as such, we would have to get special permission. "But," he added with a twinkle in his eye, "after all, one could use some discretion." We assume he meant that the occasional picture would be overlooked.

Inside, however, we didn't see too much that could be photographed on a casual tour. The rooms are huge and impressive, but not at all colorful. We decided that the outside views were much better.

There is one good inside shot of the huge **ASTRONOMICAL CLOCK**, which you can shoot in the inner courtyard. It faces east, so it's in the sun in the morning and shaded in the afternoon.

When to go

The lighting can be a problem on your photo tour of Hampton Court. The orientation is east and west, which means that you'll have good sun on the garden side of the building in the morning and good light on the main entrance in the afternoon. On Sunday afternoon the gardens open at 2 P.M. (Other days they are open at 9:30 A.M.) We recommend Sunday afternoon because there are many visitors and you have the further opportunity of taking candids of Britishers strolling around in their Sunday best, or informally picnicking on the grounds. Additionally, the afternoon tour is better than the morning for the light. You can take good shots in the gardens, and the better outside view of the building on the west side, which is lighted by the afternoon sun.

8. Conclusion

We have told you about *our* London and how to shoot the pictures we've selected. But you will find *your* London and other subjects to shoot when you go.

Keep in mind that if you choose subjects other than those listed here, you can still use the information in this book by referring to a similar subject that we have suggested, or check the "Tips and Techniques" section for useful "how to" picture-taking procedures.

On the average, most tourists stay in London for three days. This isn't all that much time for seeing, much less picturing, one of the world's greatest cities. We have kept this "short stay" in mind in organizing this book and have put the best pictorial sights first; so if your visit is a typically brief one, you can start at the beginning and follow through as you go along.

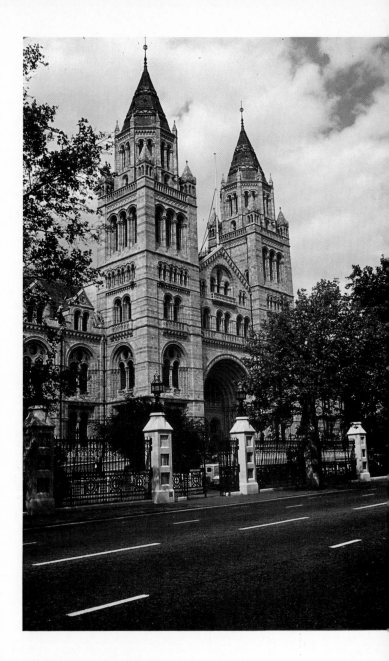

The twin towers of the Museum
of Natural History can best be
photographed from across the
Brompton Road with the camera held vertically.

Tips and Techniques

The tips and techniques listed in this section are based on extensive on-assignment travel photography experience. They deal with particular picture problems referred to in the text. This section will also serve as a field guide to special photographic questions that might arise during your travels.

ASA—WHAT IT IS AND HOW TO USE IT

The ASA number on your film package tells you how sensitive the emulsion is to light. The lower the number, such as ASA 25, the less sensitive the film is to light; the higher the number, such as ASA 400, the more sensitive it is.

Photographers refer to this light-sensitivity as the "speed" of the film and refer to the film as "slow" (a low-numbered ASA) or "fast" (a high-numbered ASA). In all cases, the slower the film the finer-grained it is and the better the color rendition and resolution. The faster films are always grainier, even if the color looks just as good.

For general shooting, choose a medium-speed film. In color, use ASA 64, and in black-and-white use ASA 100 for best all-around results.

If you are very particular or you want to have big enlargements made from your negatives or transparencies, then use the slow emulsions like Kodachrome 25 for color, and Panatomic-X for black-and-white.

There are times when you need a fast film because you want to photograph in low light levels, or to stop action. Then you should change to a film with an ASA of 200 or higher.

Each time you double the ASA of the film, you can close your lens down one stop, or use the next higher shutter speed. For example, if your exposure on ASA 64 film is f/4 at 1/30 sec., by changing to ASA 125 film, you can either stop down nearly to f/5.6, or increase the shutter speed to 1/60 sec. and open up slightly from f/4.

ASA–DIN CONVERSION CHART

ASA AND DIN FILM SPEEDS

ASA	DIN	ASA	DIN	ASA	DIN	ASA	DIN
6	9	25	15	100	21	400	27
8	10	32	16	125	22	500	28
10	11	40	17	160	23	640	29
12	12	50	18	200	24	800	30
16	13	64	19	250	25	1000	31
20	14	80	20	320	26	1250	32

BRACKETING

Bracketing is insurance to make certain that you get a good exposure. The pros use this technique, and you should too when you're in doubt about your exposure.

The procedure is first, to make an exposure as your meter indicates. Then, make additional exposures over and under your meter reading. How many additional exposures you need for insurance depends on the subject; but usually two over and two under will give you a good bracket.

You can change either the shutter speeds or the f-stops when you bracket. The choice depends on whether you want to keep the f-stop for sharpness, or the shutter speed to stop motion. For example, if your basic exposure is f/8 at 1/30 sec., to keep your depth of field, increase your exposures by changing shutter speeds down to 1/15 sec. or 1/8 sec., or up to 1/60 sec. or 1/125 sec. instead of changing your f-stop. If, on the other hand, you want to maintain the shutter speed to stop movement, then change your f-stop down to f/5.6 or f/4, or up to f/11 or f/16.

Use the bracketing technique when you don't have a meter, when the light is too low to get a reading, or when the subject is too far away to meter.

Silhouettes often make powerful compositions. This view across the Thames of Queen Boadicea's statue is effective in color or black and white. Be sure to expose for the sky to capture a dark silhouette.

CANDIDS AND CHANCE ENCOUNTERS

There are some pictures that you do not anticipate or cannot set up; they are the ones that just happen and you have to be prepared to take them when they do.

Chance Encounters
The technique for photographing the unexpected is to be prepared beforehand.

To be prepared for chance encounters, preset your shutter speed at 1/125 sec., take a light reading, and adjust your f-stop accordingly. Set your lens focus to the distance at which you most frequently take pictures—say 15 feet. This way, as you are touring and walking around between sights, when you see a passing scene, you can just raise your camera to your eye and shoot.

Candids
Candids of people in action, like a peddler selling umbrellas from a pushcart on a rainy day, also call for camera preparation. In this case, focus on your subject, set your shutter speed and f-stop, wait for the right moment, and shoot.

It takes practice to shoot candids and to take advantage of chance encounters. Don't be discouraged if you miss some; keep trying.

CHANGING FILM IN MIDROLL

Sometimes, after you have begun to shoot a roll of film, a new picture opportunity occurs that calls for a different kind of film. These new pictures do not have to be missed because you don't want to lose the unexposed part of the film in your camera. You can change your film and reshoot the roll later.

The way to do this is to note the number of the last exposed frame and rewind the film, stopping just short of pulling the leader back into the cassette. You will know when the film is off the take-up spool, because there will be a sudden loosening up of the tension. At that time, take the film out and write the number of the last exposure on the leader.

When you want to finish the started roll, insert it into the camera as you normally do, cover up the lens with the lens cap, or your hand, and click off the exposed number of shots, plus one. (The extra one is your insurance that you are past the exposed section.) Then you can go ahead and finish shooting the remainder of the roll.

COLOR SATURATION

The ideal color transparency is just on the edge of under-exposure so that it has as much detail in the highlight areas as possible. This kind of transparency is said to have full color saturation.

The easiest way to achieve this kind of exposure is to increase your ASA rating by one-half stop. This means that with ASA 25 film, you would set your ASA dial for 32 instead of 25. This can be done because there is a built-in safety factor in the ASA rating of films; you can be a little underexposed, or a little overexposed, and still get a good exposure.

If you reset your ASA for full color saturation, you have to be extra careful with your metering because you no longer have the safety factor. Unless you are very practiced, this system is not appropriate for general shooting. But you can still use it on occasion, by making an extra exposure one-half stop down from your meter reading if you think the picture would be improved by full color saturation.

Underexposed Distant Scenes

When taking distant views, a good rule of thumb is to underexpose from one-half to one full stop from your meter reading. This will give better and deeper color saturation in the highlights —the light parts of the scene.

CUSTOMS (UNITED STATES)

If you are leaving from the States, register your camera equipment—that means bodies, lenses, and all accessories—with the U.S. Customs Office at your local airport or point of departure. You have to take your gear there and have it personally verified as to description and serial number; and fill out Form 4457 (long) or Form 4455 (short) on all items you are taking out of the country. The purpose of this registration is so that you can prove on your return that you did not buy the equipment overseas.

Call your local Customs Office to find out when and where this can be done. In most large airports the registration offices are open from 8 A.M. to midnight, so you can go at your convenience before departure instead of waiting for the last-minute rush.

When you register your equipment, be sure to pick up the latest list of import duties and restrictions on trademarked equipment that you can legally bring back. This list will be useful if you plan to purchase photographic equipment overseas, because it shows the amount of import duty you will have to pay. These duties vary; lenses are currently assessed at 15 percent and camera bodies at 7.5 percent.

The trademark import restrictions apply to some brands of cameras imported to the United States. You can only bring back a limited number of these cameras and lenses, even if you did pay for them overseas and are willing to pay the import duties on your return.

DEVELOPING FILMS

When you have taken an unusually large number of photographs far away from home, you will want to take great care when the time comes to develop them. Here are some practical precautions. If you send your films out to be processed:

- do not send them all at once, but in 4 or 5 batches
- divide the batches to include different places and times
- have the first batch developed and view the results before you have any more done. (Although it is rare, machines do break down in commercial labs, so it is safer not to have all your films in at one time. This method also gives you the chance to ask the lab to compensate in future rolls if you notice that you were consistently over- or underexposing.)
- have the rest of the batches processed at separate times.

If you develop the films yourself:

- again, divide the rolls into batches
- do not try any new processes — use the method you know and are comfortable with
- use fresh chemicals
- run a test roll—maybe even two
- when you are satisfied with the test results run the rest of the films through, a few at a time.

These precautions will make you wait a little longer to see your results, but the insurance they offer is more than worthwhile.

DOUBLE EXPOSURES

Double exposures can be achieved in two ways: You can take them in the camera or you can sandwich slides together and copy them onto another slide.

To make double exposures in the camera, you have to be able either to stop the film from advancing so that you can make another exposure on the same frame, or to rewind the film accurately so that the next exposure fits over the previous exposure. With some 35 mm cameras you can simply depress the rewind-lock button (usually on the bottom of the camera) while making a succession of exposures, because then the advance lever will cock the shutter but not pull the film through. With other models you must first shoot, then rewind the film normally one full revolution, and then shoot again.

When you are double exposing in the camera you will need to underexpose one stop for each exposure you make, unless one of your photographs has a dark area into which you plan to place a lighter subject for the next exposure. In this case you can expose normally for both.

If you intend to sandwich slides together later, you should plan for it by overexposing the photographs when you take them so that the final result will not be too dark.

Sandwiching slides together does have the advantage that you can do it on a light table and see what effect you are getting. When you double expose in the camera you cannot always be sure that your subjects are lined up correctly.

Sometimes a close-up of a detail can make an interesting picture. Such was the case with this fresh order of fish and chips.

EQUIPMENT—CHOOSING WHAT YOU WANT

Choosing cameras, lenses, and accessories is a highly personal affair. What works for one photographer may not suit another. The way to choose your photographic equipment is first to decide the *kind* of pictures you want to take, and how much of your energy is going to be put into photography.

You should also consider what *kind* of photographer you are. If you're the type who only wants to take the occasional picture—with a minimum of fuss—to show where you've been, then the simplest camera will do; preferably the one you now have, because you are already familiar with it. If you are an avid snapshooter and have a greater interest in picture-taking and want to shoot enough for a good album display or a slide show, then you will need more equipment. Finally, if you are really serious about photography, and are an advanced amateur, semi-professional, or professional, you will want enough equipment for outstanding pictures, and different equipment for each type of picture-taking situation.

110 Cameras

For the first category, the simplest and easiest cameras to use are the popular, pocket-sized **110 CAMERAS**. They are now produced by a number of different manufacturers at prices ranging from $20 to over $200.

The desirable features on these are the zoom-telephoto lens and the built-in electronic flash.

New 110 cameras are now also on the market with interchangeable lenses and all the features of the 35 mm single-lens reflex (SLR) cameras. You should look at these if size and weight are a travel consideration.

The miniature 110 is suitable for snapshot-size enlargements, photo-album displays, and projection with the new 110 projectors.

Rangefinder Cameras

For the step up into more serious *35 mm* photography, you have a choice between the rangefinder and the SLR types.

Of these, the simpler and less expensive are the **RANGEFINDER CAMERAS** that come with a fixed lens in the 40 mm range, which gives a slight wide-angle result. These are fine for all-around shooting, but you will tire of them after a while because you can't change the lens and there isn't much room for creativity.

The price range on these simple 35 mm cameras is comparable to the 110's, and they are a better investment if you want image quality rather than portability.

The SLR Camera System

The obvious choice over the fixed-lens rangefinder 35 mm camera is the single-lens reflex (SLR). Through-the-lens viewing shows the picture exactly as you're going to take it, and technology has brought these cameras down to a size and weight that is comparable to that of the rangefinders. Because the SLR is such a popular camera, you have a wide range of choice in features, lenses, and price. But a little common sense will help you make a decision.

Ask yourself, "What am I going to do with the pictures?" "How far into photography am I, and how far do I plan to go?" If the pictures are for yourself and not for the competitive photo market and if you plan to make only normal (that is, up to 16″ × 20″ enlargements), then you could settle for any of the less-expensive competitive brands. If you can define your aims in photography and know that you'll be satisfied with good results from a limited number of lenses, then you don't have to go for the line that has the most options.

A good way to start an SLR system is to buy the body only (without the 50 mm normal lens that comes with it) and a wide-angle and a telephoto lens. The 50 mm is the one that you will use the least; you will always want to go wider or longer, so why not start out that way?

A good all-purpose wide-angle that will even double for the 50 mm is a 35 mm lens. A moderate telephoto that is just right for portraits and general shooting is the 85 mm lens. We recommend these two as a start.

Of course, you have other options. If you keep the 50 mm, then you should buy a wide-angle lens of 28 mm or an even wider-angle 24 mm. You could also increase the range of the telephoto up to 105 mm or 135 mm. Or, you can opt for a zoom lens and have a combination of focal lengths in one lens. This is an advantage, and a zoom lens is fun because you can frame your image as desired at any focal length without moving toward or away from your subject.

For the serious picture-taker, the sky is the limit, and we won't even talk about price. Here is where the lens options really start. The trick, however, is to buy slowly, before you are over your head. After you have the gear recommended for the intermediates, choose each succeeding item carefully and think of the use you will make of it before you buy.

When expanding your lens system, keep in mind two lenses that are real workhorses: the 20 mm wide-angle and the 200 mm telephoto. The 20 mm wide-angle lens is great for interiors because it's the last stop before you get to the line-bending fisheyes, and the 200 mm telephoto lens is the most practical handholdable focal-length lens for those long shots.

Besides the extra lenses, you should consider an extra camera body. This has many advantages. It will enable you:

- to keep two kinds of film loaded

- to have two bodies ready for fast shooting with a lens on each

- to have an extra camera if something should go wrong.

Accessories

Besides the camera equipment, you should have the following accessories:

- A good *tabletop tripod*. (Get one that is really sturdy; it's worth the extra money.)

- Basic *filters* needed for color photography: a **1A SKYLIGHT** filter to warm up scenes with excessive blue, such as aerials, snow scenes, and overcast cloudy daylight; a **POLARIZING** filter to eliminate reflections, cut down glare, and darken a blue sky without changing the color of the scene; an **80A** filter to convert daylight film to tungsten; an **85B** filter to change tungsten film to daylight; and a **TIFFEN FLD** filter to correct fluorescent light on daylight film and an **FLB** filter to do the same on indoor tungsten emulsion. We also recommend that you keep a **UV** (ultraviolet light absorption) filter on each lens to protect it from dirt and scratches. This filter won't affect the color or exposure. (See itemized filter list in this section.)

- A small *jeweler's screwdriver* is useful for those occasionally loose screws. (The blade of a Swiss Army knife can be honed down to a small screwdriver size.)

- A small plastic bottle of *lens-cleaning fluid* and a packet of *lens-cleaning tissues* are essential. In addition, carry a *lens brush* to flick off the dust. It is not a good idea to rub the lens too much; you might damage the lens coating.

- A small, simple strobe *flash unit* that you can carry in your gadget bag should answer your flash needs. This will do for the occasional flash shot, and this book will tell you how to take pictures in practically all situations without flash where you may have thought that flash was indispensable (see "Flash—When and How to Use It" in this section).

- At this stage, you have to consider a *gadget bag*. It should hold all of your equipment, all of your accessories, plus have some room left over for film, maps, a notebook, and this book. It's a good idea to take all your gear with you when you go bag shopping to see if it all fits before you buy.

There is a bottom line on equipment that may help you keep it in perspective: remember that equipment alone is not going to get you the picture. Only *you* can choose what you see and direct your camera to take it.

EQUIPMENT CHECKLIST FOR TRAVEL PHOTOGRAPHY

You should take the following equipment with you to cover all the picture possibilities explained in this book.

Camera

- We recommend an SLR camera that will accept interchangeable lenses.

Lenses

- A 35 mm lens for general shooting (or a 50 mm lens)

- A 24 mm wide-angle lens (or a 28 mm lens)

- An 85 mm medium-telephoto lens (or one up to 105 mm). (In addition, you can substitute a zoom lens that covers these focal lengths or adds to them.)

Filters

- 1A skylight filter

- Polarizing filter

- 80A and 85B conversion filters

- Tiffen FLD and FLB fluorescent-light correction filters

- UV (ultraviolet absorption) filters

- Additionally, for black-and-white photography, a K-2 yellow, an orange, and a red filter.

Tripods

- You'll get by with a tabletop tripod, but get a sturdy one.

Accessories

- Lens-cleaning brush

- Lens-cleaning fluid

- Jeweler's screwdriver or substitute

- Cable release for long exposures.

Gadget Bag

- Get this last and see if all your gear fits. Don't buy one that looks so ostentatious that it screams, "there is valuable equipment inside!"

Film

- The bulk of your film needs should be covered by a medium-speed color film, like Kodachrome 64, or its equivalent in other brands.

- Extra film should be Ektachrome 200 and 400 film (daylight) for outdoor dim light and indoor daylight shooting, and Ektachrome 160 film (tungsten) for indoor photography.

- Added to this, you can take some rolls of Tri-X black-and-white film. Substitutions can be negative color films, such as Kodacolor II (ASA 100), or Kodacolor 400 film.

- To estimate film needs, multiply your anticipated normal day use from past experience by the number of shooting days on the trip.

EXPOSURE

Exposure is one of the greatest problems in photography. No matter how accurate your meter is, or how automated the camera, there are always exceptions in determining the right exposure.

Exposure meters are calibrated to give you the best reading for the middle tones of the average scene. This means that the exposure reading for the frontlighted picture will be accurate, and you will get maximum tonal values of light and dark according to the capability of the film. But if you are up against an "unaverage" lighting situation, the meter gets confused and you have to help it out.

Backlighted or sidelighted scenes, or landscapes with large areas of dark and light, such as sky or snow, will throw your light meter off. You will get a correct reading for the lightest areas, but the rest of your picture will be underexposed. In these situations you can still enlist the aid of your meter to give you correct exposure, but you have to direct it to give you the information you want.

If a person is backlighted and you want detail in the face, move in close with your meter to cut out the backlight, and take your reading off the face. If you want a silhouette against the setting sun, then point the meter at the sunset and let the figure go black.

The same is true of beach scenes with large areas of light reflecting sand, and of snow scenes with blinding white landscapes. Again, you have to decide what you want to say with your picture and meter accordingly.

In a beach scene, if you want the texture of the golden grains of sand, take a reading of the sand; if you want the figure under the beach umbrella, then direct your meter under the umbrella. The same holds true for snow scenes: To capture the sheen of light reflected off the white snow surface, you must meter exactly that; to show the features of your friend skiing, move in close and determine the exposure for the figure. In each case you have to decide which part of the picture is the most important and make your exposure there.

Warning: Be especially careful in determining exposure for scenes where a light source is shining directly into the lens. Sunsets and spotlighted show scenes are especially difficult. The solution is to move the lens view so that the light source does not shine into the lens but just off to the side. Take the meter reading from this just-out-of-the-light view then swing back for your original composition.

To give variety to your pictures, add a close-up object to complement the background scene. A wide-angle lens of 28 mm enlarged the foreground cannon and diminished the guardsman in this Tower of London scene.

FILM

Choice of film is just as highly personal as the choice of cameras and lenses. But there are some guidelines. You should choose your film, as you choose your camera and lenses, with the end product in mind: your pictures and what you want from them.

If you are shooting a subject that calls for sharpness, or critical color balance, then you should use the slower, fine-grain films. But if you are going after mood or action in poor light, then you need fast films, or those that can be pushed.

Unfortunately, when you're traveling and moving from place to place, you can't predict your film needs. Therefore, you should take a balanced assortment of film along with you. It can be distressing to have a picture possibility before you and not have the right film in your gadget bag.

We carry Kodachrome 64, Agfachrome 64, Ektachrome 200 and 400 (daylight), Ektachrome 160 (tungsten), and Tri-X black-and-white film in our gadget bags at all times.

The Kodachrome and Agfachrome films are for general shooting and account for 90 percent of the pictures.

The Ektachrome 200 and 400 films (daylight) are for dim-light shooting at dusk, for shooting in poor weather, and for night pictures in order to stop the movement of cars and people.

Ektachrome 160 film (tungsten) is for indoor use at shows, theaters, nightclubs, and places where artificial lights are used. We routinely double the ASA of this film, which makes practically all indoor-lighted situations possible without flash.

Tri-X is a good all-purpose film, in case we want to shoot some black-and-white pictures. With careful development, this film gives reproduction-quality enlargements.

On a trip, it's best to use both film and equipment that you have already tested. Don't experiment while you're traveling, because you may not be able to repeat some of the shots.

FILTERS AND HOW TO USE THEM

Some filters help to counteract certain light conditions in a photograph. There are others which can be used for special effects.

Correction Filters
In the first category are the filters that we have listed in the equipment section.

- The UV (ultraviolet absorption) filter to protect your lenses

- The polarizing filter to cut glare and increase contrast

- The 80A filter to correct daylight color emulsion to tungsten lighting

- The 85B filter to correct tungsten film to daylight

- The two filters to correct fluorescent light: an FLD for daylight film and an FLB for tungsten film.

None of these filters alters the color; rather they correct it, so that the picture will appear natural.

Special-Effects Filters

The second category of filters—for special effects—includes so many that a catalog is needed to classify them. These comprise not only the color tint filters, but those for prism effects, split fields, star effects, and many others. You can play around with these filters and they are fun, but you may not have much time on a trip to experiment. It is far better to try these special effects before leaving. Then if some of the filters appeal to you, take them along and use them for certain effects you might want. A star filter, for example, can come in very handy for candlelighted scenes.

You can also use some of the filters made for black-and-white correction with color film. When the sky is gray, for example, and you want an orange sunset, you can manufacture one by using an orange or red filter.

The thing to remember about filters is: Don't use one unless you really need to, because filter glass never measures up to lens optics and you will lose some sharpness.

FLASH—WHEN AND HOW TO USE IT

There are times when flash is absolutely necessary; there are other times when it will help; and there are occasions when, unfortunately, it is used but is not needed or is completely useless.

Flash *is necessary* when there is not enough light to shoot by, or when you want to stop action in poor light. But you must remember that each flash unit can throw its light only a certain distance. Beyond that distance your subject will not be illuminated. The flash's carrying power depends on the strength of the unit and the speed (the ASA rating) of the film that you are using. The stronger the light, which usually means the heavier the unit, the farther it will light the scene; and the higher the ASA rating of the film, the more sensitive it is to the light output. So by changing to a faster film, you can get more "light" out of your flash.

It's easy to determine the exposure for your flash shots. You can use the guide number (G.N.) or a flash with an automatic system. The automatic system is easier, because the unit does most of the work. All you have to do is to choose the *f*-stop that falls within the range of the distance you are from the subject, and the unit will measure out the exact light needed when you flash.

The guide-number system takes a little mathematics. First you have to know the G.N. of your unit with the film that you are using, because the G.N. changes with the ASA rating. Then, divide the G.N. by the distance, in feet, that you are from the subject. Finally, set the *f*-stop to the nearest number corresponding to this result. Following is an example of how this works: If the G.N. for your flash is 80 with Ektachrome 200 or 400 film and you are 10 feet from your subject, then you would divide 80 by 10, with a result of 8. The 8 would then be converted to *f*/8 as the setting for your picture.

Whichever system you use, always be sure that your shutter setting is on the *sync* speed for your flash so that you don't get a partially exposed frame.

Flash with Daylight

Flash can be used to help out a daylight scene that is unevenly lighted, such as an indoor-outdoor scene where you want to see the people inside and the view of the outside. To take a picture like this, you have to do some calculating.

First set your shutter on *sync* speed for your camera (usually 1/60 sec.). Then take a meter reading of the outside scene through the window and set your *f*-stop for that. To balance this with the light from your flash, divide the *f*-stop of your outside reading into the G.N. of your flash. This will give you the distance in feet for correct flash exposure. Take your combination flash-daylight scene from this distance and both your indoor flash scene and your outdoor background will be correctly exposed.

Flash with Indoor Lighting

The color and exposure of interior scenes with indoor lighting can also be helped by the addition of flash. The technique for figuring the exposure is similar to the combination daylight-flash shots.

If you would like to illuminate your subject with flash but would also like to have glowing lamps showing, then shoot at the calculated flash *f*-stop setting but slow your shutter speed down to 1/15 sec., or for more glow, to 1/8 sec. You should get a good overall flash exposure and the added slow shutter speed will register the lamplight. This makes a very pleasing picture, because the warm glow of the lights adds a natural look.

You can also use flash to correct the color balance of the light when you are using outdoor film *indoors,* so that you don't have to use a filter. To do this, first take a meter reading of the interior. Next, stop down one-half to one stop, depending on the size of the room. When shooting, bounce your flash off the ceiling or a wall. This procedure will correct the color balance of the indoor light on outdoor film, and the additional light from the flash will also give the correct exposure.

When you shoot this combination of flash and existing light, the interior lighting on outdoor color film will be warm but not the blood-red color you normally would get.

It is best to bracket and make additional shots when using both of these techniques so that you have a choice among the results.

When Not to Use Flash

The first and most obvious useless use of flash is when you are sitting in the upper rows of a stadium and expect to take an exposure of the distant scene below with a peanut-size flashbulb or a "lightning-bug" output strobe unit. This cannot be done. Just check the instructions with your unit and you'll see that the light won't reach far enough.

Another time not to flash is when the lighting is strong enough to take pictures by available light. Stage shows, night-club acts, and other illuminated scenes can be photographed with a fast, tungsten film. The resulting photo will be better than a flat flash picture, because it will show the dramatic lighting that makes the scene interesting.

Flash for portraits is unsatisfactory because it produces a harsh flat light that either washes out the features or accentuates the flaws. If you must use flash, it is best to soften the effect by bouncing the flash off the wall or ceiling. For bounced light, open up two stops from normal flash exposure to compensate for the added distance.

Generally, the best policy is not to use flash unless you must.

FOCUSING—GENERAL RULES

If you are in doubt when focusing on a scene and want the whole scene to be in focus, pick an object or person about one third of the distance into the picture and use it as your focus point. This rule of thumb will give you the most depth of field.

Where there is a dominant subject, focus directly on your center of interest and do not worry about the rest of the scene.

Selective Focus

A good way to get rid of bothersome and busy backgrounds is to open your lens to a larger *f*-stop so that your depth of field is short and the background goes blurry. How much you open the lens depends on the depth of your subject, and the way to judge the effect is to look at the image with the depth-of-field preview button depressed. (If your camera doesn't have one, you'll have to approximate by using your depth-of-field scale. Usually, your calculations do not have to be critically accurate.) If you open up to stops of *f*/4 or larger, move in close to your subject, and compensate for the larger lens opening by increasing your shutter speed. Your background will disappear into a nice blur.

Blurring out the background is especially effective when taking portraits. Not only will the larger opening give a more pleasing focus on the face (be sure to focus right on the iris of the eye in full-face portraits), but because you are close up to your subject the background will be even more out of focus.

Selective focus is a good technique to use for portrait close-ups. By shooting with a moderate telephoto lens (80 mm to 135 mm) and opening up to apertures of f/2.8 to f/4, you can get the effect of large-format professional portraiture. The longer-focal-length lens and the large lens opening on a 35 mm format will approximate the "sharp eyes and soft-focus look" of the larger cameras and longer-focal-length portrait lenses.

Focusing with the Depth-of-Field Scale

The depth-of-field scale markings on the barrel of your lens show the near and far limits of what is in focus at the different f-stop settings.

These marks are located at the top of your lens. To use them, first focus your lens on the subject. Next, look at the depth-of-field marks for the f-stop you are using, and check these against the distance marks to see how near and how far the zone of sharp focus extends. This will be your *depth of field*. It is useful to know what depth of field you have when photographing moving subjects, or in determining how much of the foreground and the background of a still subject is sharp.

A word on moving subjects. It is impossible to focus accurately on moving subjects. So instead of sharp focusing, you can "guesstimate" the distance by setting your focus between the depth-of-field marks on your lens. This way if the subject moves closer, or farther away, you will still be in focus. This system will only work for normal and wide-angle lenses.

The depth-of-field scale is also useful when you want to shoot a scene with maximum depth of field. This might be a street scene, a scenic with a person or an object in the foreground, or an interior of a long room or a building; in other words, a situation where your subject has depth and where you want everything equally sharp. For such scenes, set the far distance marker for the f-stop you're using on infinity. The near distance marker for that stop will show you where this maximum depth of field begins. This technique is especially effective with wide-angle lenses where your image can be sharp as close as 3 feet and as far as infinity. By doing this you are, in effect, focusing at one-third of the distance into the scene.

Prefocusing for Action

Prefocusing is a way of taking pictures of moving subjects and making sure that they will be sharp.

The method is to focus on a spot that your subject will have to cross, and to shoot the picture when the subject arrives at that spot. This works especially well when taking candids of people walking. Look ahead so that you can see your subject coming; decide how close you want to take the picture; and focus on just about anything on that spot. It can be a crack in the pavement, a curb edge on a street crossing, or a light pole or object that your subject will have to pass.

A shutter speed of 1/125 sec. is sufficient to stop the action of subjects walking toward you, but if they are running, or if the angle is from the side, 1/250 sec. or even 1/500 sec. is safer.

Prefocusing is the system that sports photographers use when covering fast-moving events. In summary, it is preframing the picture area before the action arrives so that you are ready to shoot instantly when your subject steps on the spot.

Focus carefully when shooting details. This Lombard Street statue is striking because of the sharpness of the image. Move in close on such scenes or use a telephoto lens to bring them up.

HIP SHOOTING

"Shooting from the hip" is a good technique to use when you want to make candid photographs of people in public places without intruding. The practice gets its name from the sharpshooters of the old-time Wild West shows.

The trick is to preset your camera for an average distance and exposure and, with the camera dangling around your neck, to keep your finger on the shutter release. When you see a situation that you want to photograph, instead of bringing the camera up to your eye, turn your body to aim at the subject, hold steady, and press the button. This system takes a little practice, but it really works — and it's fun. You should use a wide-angle lens if you can because your framing won't be exact and you'll need the additional depth of field that a short focal length gives. Remember that you don't have to be focused exactly. Check the scale on your lens to see how much depth of field you have at the *f*-stop you are using.

Candid shots such as this, of a street musician in front of Westminster Abbey, are best taken when the action is natural. Use this prefocusing technique: first, focus on the scene; then, lower your camera and watch for the action you want; when you see it, quickly raise the camera to eye level and shoot.

INSURANCE

Check with your insurance agent to be sure that all of your cameras, lenses, and accessories are insured for your trip abroad. This is a good time to make certain that your equipment is fully insured at *all* times.

If your home insurance doesn't cover your gear, then take out a camera floater on your present policy. This costs a little more, but may save you a major investment in replacing lost or stolen equipment.

If you have a great deal of equipment, you may have to take out a special policy, since most household insurance plans only cover a minimum, such as one camera with one or two lenses.

INTERIOR SHOOTING

The chief difference between indoor and outdoor picture-taking is that indoors you need more exposure to compensate for the poorer light. Because of this need for a longer exposure, you often have to support your camera. Usually this is best done with a tripod, but when traveling, such a heavy piece of equipment is cumbersome to carry around. (A good substitute is a small tabletop tripod that will fit into your gadget bag, or pocket for that matter.)

Another problem indoors is that sometimes you cannot back up far enough to get your subject into the frame. A wide-angle lens is the solution to this problem. There are several focal lengths to choose from: a 35 mm which is acceptable for most situations, a 28 mm which is usually sufficient, and a 24 mm which will always work. Of course, there are times when a normal 50 mm lens will take in your scene.

Besides supporting your camera and using a wide-angle lens, if the scene is lighted by tungsten light rather than daylight, you must either use a tungsten-balanced film or adapt your daylight film by use of a conversion filter. Ektachrome 160 film (tungsten) works very well in interiors illuminated by light bulbs, spotlights, or even candlelight. You can also use daylight film with an 80A conversion filter.

Some interiors are illuminated by fluorescent lighting. This kind of light produces a sickly green color on any film. To correct this off color, you should use a correction filter like the Tiffen FLD for daylight film or the FLB for tungsten film.

Don't be afraid to take interior shots. Just find a convenient doorway, wall, or column against which you can support your camera and keep it plumb both vertically and horizontally so that your picture is not crooked. (For a description of how to make these supported exposures, see "Tripod and Tripod-less Exposures.")

METRIC CONVERSION INFORMATION

When You Know	Multiply by	To Find
inches (in.)	25.4	millimetres (mm)
feet (ft.)	0.3048	metres (m)
miles (mi.)	1.609	kilometres (km)
ounces (oz.)	28.349	grams (g)
pounds (lbs.)	0.453	kilograms (kg)
pounds per square inch (psi.)	0.0703	kilograms per square centimetre (kg/sqcm)
cubic feet (cu. ft.)	0.0283	cubic meters
Fahrenheit temperature (F)	0.5556 after subtracting 32	Celsius temperature (C)

MUSEUMS

When photography is permitted, museums make great picture-hunting grounds. You can take good slide copies of the paintings you admire in the museums where photography is permitted and you don't have to use a flash or a tripod. You can use a fast daylight color film, such as Ektachrome 200 or 400, which can be shot at the rated film speed, or pushed to a faster ASA. To determine whether to push the film, take an exposure reading of one of the darker paintings. If you can shoot at f/2.8 at 1/30 sec., then you can use the rated ASA. If not, keep doubling the ASA on your meter, or, if you have a through-the-lens meter, the ASA dial of your camera, until you can shoot at the above setting.

You can safely double the ASA of Ektachrome film from 200 to 400 without much loss in film quality. It can be further pushed to 800, but that requires very special handling. The trick is never to push film unless you must; and if you have a good camera technique and a steady hand, you should be able to open up to f/2 and be steady at 1/15 sec.

Remember, if you push a film roll at the beginning, then you have to shoot the entire roll at that ASA; you can't change your mind and start pushing in midroll. (See "Pushing Film.")

When taking the picture, be sure that you are lined up directly in front of the painting and that you are holding the camera level, both horizontally and vertically, or you may not get the whole painting in focus. Remember to turn your camera to the vertical format for vertical pictures so that you will get a full-size image.

If you are not familiar with the artist or the work, take an extra close-up shot of the nameplate as a reminder.

You can also shoot displays, but be careful of the lighting. If a display is spotlighted, use high-speed tungsten film. This can be pushed just like daylight film.

Be sure to mark all pushed rolls of film with the ASA number that you used and advise the lab when you send it in for processing.

The British Museum offers many chances for close-ups of art and artifacts. If the lighting is fluorescent, be sure to use a corrective filter (FLD for daylight color film, and FLB for tungsten).

NIGHT SHOOTING

Night shooting is strictly a matter of time exposures for which a tripod or other support is needed (see "Tripod and Tripod-less Exposures.")

The easiest and best time to take "night" pictures is not at night, but at dusk. This is the time of day when the building outlines can still be seen against the sky, and the bright inside lights as well as the street illumination are turned on. At this time exposure determination is easy; just take a straight meter reading of the scene and shoot. Be sure to use a tripod or some other support for sharpness.

Determining the proper exposure is more difficult at night, because bare-light readings throw the meter off, giving you the exposure for the existing light sources, not the lighted scene itself. To get a correct overall reading, take the metered reading from an illuminated area, not from the light bulb itself; or figure an average between your high and low readings for the correct setting.

No matter how accurately you try to meter night scenes, there will be some discrepancy because of *reciprocity failure*. (This simply means that most film is not made for long exposures; therefore, you can't tell how it is going to behave.) So, rather than get up-tight about your exposures, just bracket (see "Bracketing").

Use daylight color film for illuminated night scenes. It gives a warm cast that offsets the blue haze of night.

If you don't have a meter or can't get a reading from the one you have, bracket on the following exposures: For fully illuminated buildings, on Ektachrome 200 film (daylight), use 1/4 sec. at *f*/2; and if you are shooting with Kodachrome 64, use 1 sec. at *f*/2. Since light conditions vary, always bracket.

Illuminated buildings make memorable night shots. Rest your camera on some sturdy object and remember to bracket your exposures.

PUSHING FILM

There are times when you will want to take pictures in low-light situations where you do not want to, or cannot, use flash. In such cases you can "push" your film by using it at a higher ASA rating than the manufacturer gives. By doing this you under-expose the whole roll of film, then compensate by having it overdeveloped when it is processed.

To push a film, set the ASA dial on your camera or exposure meter to a higher number than the one marked on the film box. The best policy is to increase the ASA rating by doubling it—for example, from 160 to 320, or 200 to 400. Each time you double the ASA rating you can shoot at one f-stop smaller (or one shutter speed faster). Hence the term to "push one stop, two stops," etc.

You can "push", or increase the speed, of most films safely up to a two-times increase (200 ASA to 800 ASA). Ektachrome can be pushed, at an added cost for processing. But if you push more than two times you will have difficulty in finding a commercial lab to process the film. Not all of them will do it. Kodachrome can be pushed only at a very high cost for processing, and very few labs will handle it. (The Eastman Kodak Company will not accept Kodachrome for push processing.)

When you push film you not only increase the speed but you also change the characteristics. In black-and-white film the grain is increased and there is loss of detail in the highlight and shadow areas. In color film, the grain is increased, blacks are lost, and there is a color shift.

Important. You must remember when you "push" a film that you have to do it for the *whole roll* and you *MUST* mark on the roll how much you increased it so that you can tell the lab how to process it.

The Natural History Museum offers colorful exhibits in the children's section. These displays are well lit and can be photographed with the available light by supporting your camera on any steady object.

SELF-TIMER USES

The primary use of a self-timer is to include yourself in a picture, but it has other uses too. You can use it to trip the shutter while you are holding the camera against a support during time exposures or when you are shooting with a long telephoto lens. (In most SLR's you can lock up the mirror and release the shutter with the self-timer to avoid vibration.)

The self-timer can also be used to trip the shutter when you want to take an overhead shot of a decorated ceiling. Simply place the camera on the floor, lens up, set the self-timer, and step out of the lens range while the shutter trips.

SHOW SHOOTING

You can take pictures of stage performances, outdoor-lighted spectacles, and even nightclub acts with the existing light.

Use Ektachrome 160 film (tungsten) and double the ASA. You can take a meter reading if there is enough sidelight to see your meter, but if you cannot, here is a guide list of exposures you can use.

- If it is average white-colored stage lighting, you can shoot tungsten film at its normal ASA at 1/30 sec. and f/4.

- If colored gels are used, the exposure can vary down to 1/15 sec. at f/2. (In this case, it is better to double or even triple the rated ASA (to 320 or 640) and shoot at 1/30 sec. at f/2.8 because it's difficult to hold the camera steady at lower shutter speeds, and lower than f/2.8, the depth of field is very shallow.)

A moderate telephoto of 85 mm to 105 mm is ideal for a large image. Don't try to take in all of the stage, unless the scenery is your point of interest, because shooting at slow shutter speeds doesn't really produce very sharp images, and you won't be able to enlarge the image very much.

Watch the action and make your exposures when a movement has just been completed, or when there is no motion. Try to click the shutter when there is a peak in the music, or other stage sound, to cover up the shutter noise.

Show shooting is a matter of practice, since the lighting changes from scene to scene, and even while you are shooting. Until you get the hang of it, and sometimes even after you do, bracket your exposure for safety (see "Bracketing").

TRIPOD AND "TRIPOD-LESS" EXPOSURES

The ideal way to make long exposures is by putting your camera on a sturdy tripod. Unfortunately, sturdy usually means heavy. A full-size tripod is a nuisance on a trip unless you are a real aficionado, or you are taking pictures for money. On the other hand, just because you are using a small camera, you should not make the mistake of using a flimsy, lightweight tripod.

The next best bet to a full-size tripod is a tabletop tripod that you can carry in your gadget bag. Even these have to be sturdy. By sturdy, we mean that when the camera is mounted on it, the tripod doesn't move *at all*. This calls for legs that are widespread enough for balance, with a ball-and-socket joint that locks rigid.

Tripod-less exposures are possible but they take great care. You *must* hold the camera against something, such as a wall, a door frame, a pole, or even a tree trunk, and trip the shutter with a cable release or the self-timer. A self-timer works for exposures up to 1 sec., but you need a cable release for longer exposures on "B" (bulb).

The ideal compromise on a trip is to take a tabletop tripod and use it on top of ledges and tables, and hold it against doorways and trees. The tabletop tripod can also be converted to a chest pod by opening up the legs and resting them on your chest to steady handheld exposures.

The gold color of this lion statue in the Tower of London armory building was enhanced by the use of daylight High Speed Ektachrome under tungsten spotlighting. The camera was supported against a column for a ½-sec. exposure without a tripod.

WET WEATHER SHOOTING

Often the best time to shoot scenes is right after a rain, because the atmosphere has been washed clean and the dust and dirt are off the foliage. Then, just when the sun is trying to break through, there is a luminous light that gives full color saturation.

It is also a time to look for reflections on the pavement and in the puddles of water.

You can also take pictures *in* the rain, but protect your camera and gadget bag by carrying along a piece of plastic to cover them. An umbrella is essential to keep the rain off the lens. One way to use an umbrella and still keep your hands free is to stick the handle down the back of your neck inside your raincoat or jacket, and wrap the camera strap around the handle, pulling it taut as you take the picture.

Don't let wet weather prevent you from taking pictures. A parade in the rain, or with the sun bursting through the clouds, can add a twist to your sunny-side coverage.

X-RAY EXPOSURE

Although there are a number of bags and containers on the market that are said to protect your films from x-rays at airport security checks, our advice is *do not subject your film to x-ray exposure*. Even if one dose of x-rays won't affect your film, additional exposure every time you have to go through security (particularly when you are making several stops on your trip) might fog your film and cause a loss of quality especially in color material. Our suggestions for traveling with film are:

- do not pack your film in the baggage to be checked into the hold

- keep your film in a separate bag (preferably of clear plastic) that can be examined with ease

- politely ask the security guards to hand-examine your film bag, and, even if they tell you that their machines will not hurt your film, be firm — if necessary ask for a supervisor

- arrive early at the security area, so that you will not be forced to rush through without personal attention

- keep smiling, and thank the guards — remember that they are there for our protection

- film should be removed from the camera because security guards usually insist that metal contraptions be x-rayed or opened for inspection. (See "Changing Film in Midroll" for tips on how to do this.)

INDEX